Into Africa

with

3 Kids, 13 Crates

and a Husband

ANN PATRAS

Book 1 of the 'Africa' series.
Also available in Large Print and as an ebook.

Table of Contents

To the late Nancy, Mev and Doris

Loved and missed by us all

Please note, this book describes my life in Zambia, based on letters written in 1980/81. It should be noted that in the interest of authenticity, conversations and observations contained in this book reflect what was said, assumed or apparent to me at that time. I am pleased to say that attitudes have changed dramatically in Africa and the world since those days.

1

"What about Zambia?"

"What?"

"How do you feel about living in Zambia?"

"Well, I can't say I've ever given it much consideration really. Where is it?"

"In Africa I think, I don't know exactly. Where's our atlas?"

I went off in search of the atlas and we both crowded over the coffee table as Ziggy, my husband of five years, searched for the page containing Zambia. We found it on page 23 in the middle of a long pointy bit of southern Africa.

"So what's going on there?" I asked

"A cobalt plant," he said, as if that explained everything.

Ziggy had spent the past couple of weeks looking for a job. His current employers had closed the division he worked in and as he had received a fair redundancy package, he had time to search around for 'the right job'. For the past three years he had worked as a site engineer in the petrochemical industry at various coastal locations around Great Britain. We lived in Burton upon Trent, about as far as anyone can get from any British coast, which meant that most weeks he went off to the site early on a Monday morning, returning on a Friday evening.

This left me a little lonesome, and in sole charge of hand-rearing our three very young children, an arrangement hardly conducive to a fulfilling married life.

When Ziggy and I decided to start a family, about a year after we got married, we had this notion to have a couple of kids close together, then a gap of two or so years, then produce two more.

Brad had been a five-weeks premature baby. The planned two year gap between him and his first sibling went for a ball of chalk when my second pregnancy materialised very quickly and I again went into labour five weeks early. This second premature arrival didn't bother me, but it put other people on the back foot.

During my pregnancy I was getting battered from the inside every which way and was sure that I was carrying twins, but my learned GP assured me that I wasn't. The fixed-date visit to the gynaecologist four weeks before due time could not dispute or confirm this notion because I gave birth a week before the appointment date. The hospital staff were rather surprised when I produced twins. I was not. But my GP sure felt like a twit when he was told Leon was born five minutes after I had given birth to Victoria.

The jump from one to three offspring in the space of 17 months soon

5

eliminated all notions of expanding the litter any further. This dramatic increase in children meant I really had my hands full, and I could foresee my life wasn't going to get any easier

Ziggy was searching for a job where he could work closer to home and help with the brood, commuting on a daily basis.

Zambia hardly seemed close to home, but then he had implied that I would be going there too. Now I wanted to know more about living in Zambia.

"Go on then, tell me about it."

"There's a company in need of a Site Manager to build a new cobalt plant," he replied, "and it looks very interesting."

A two-year contract was on offer and the successful applicant would be provided with a house, company car, medical facilities, private education for children (when they were old enough), payment of water, electricity and telephone bills and a house servant. On top of all that there was a salary too!

"That's not too shoddy," I said.

"And," he went on, "it would mean I could be home for lunch every day."

Well, that sold it for me, I can tell you. And the prospect of having my husband at home each day after work was such an appealing thought that I think I would have moved to the South Pole if he'd asked.

"There's only one problem though," I sighed.

"What's that?"

"My mum and dad. Nancy and Mev are hardly going to welcome this news. We would be depriving them not only of their only daughter, but their only grandchildren too. And goodness knows what my grandmother Doris will have to say about it. You know how she adores 'helping' me with the kids."

"Mmm." He contemplated that one for a while. "But you know they are always very busy running their pub, and if I were to get a job up at the far reaches of Scotland, that's a long way too. And at least in Africa it should be sunny."

"That's not fair! You know sunshine is my weak spot. But you're right. And two years isn't *that* long, I expect they could visit us for a holiday."

We sat quietly for a while, lost in thought.

"What about the kids?" I asked.

"Oh, we take them with us, of course."

"No, you idiot, I mean, do you think they'll be okay with this?"

"Well, they're rather young to have an opinion, but I imagine they'll love it. You know how much they enjoy playing outside. They should be able to do that all the time over there."

"Right. Okay."

"So you think I should apply then?"

"Most definitely," I said, suddenly sitting up straight, "it could be quite interesting."

Oh boy, was that ever the understatement of the century.

6

The reaction from our relatives and friends when we told them Ziggy had been offered the post in Zambia was one of incredulity. That of my parents, Nancy and Mev was as predicted. It was not at the top of their list of 'things we would most like to see happen in 1980'. However they did understand our situation and gave us their full support, albeit with heavy hearts.

Prior to taking on their pub, my parents were involved full time in running what was originally my grandmother's very busy, street corner grocery store. In fact I was born into the business and was serving customers (no self-service in those days) as soon as I was big enough to jump up and greet them from the other side of the counter. The familiarity of the business, as well as our family's general relaxed attitude, encouraged me to call my parents, and even my grandmother, by their first names as I grew older. I only mention this to clarify that this unusual practice was by no means a sign of disrespect, but just the way we worked.

The weeks which followed were filled with pandemonium as we arranged with an Estate Agent for our house to be rented in our absence, sorted out what was to be put in storage, and crated up the things we needed to take.

Whilst all this was going on, the children were getting excited although they didn't really know why.

Eventually the big day arrived. There were lots of tears, and that was just saying goodbye to our house and the neighbours!

Several cars belonging to family and friends were used to ferry the five of us, together with our substantial luggage, to Birmingham airport. The extent of our entourage was such that the airport staff initially thought we were celebrities.

As we checked in for our fight to Heathrow I was, for the first time, beginning to feel a little nervous. My composure was not assisted by the kids' shrieks of delight at the prospect of their first flight on an aeroplane. How do you explain to three miniature tearaways that it is not the done thing to go racing off to the aircraft in preference to kissing their Nanny and Grandad goodbye for the last time in two years?

As we walked away from all the loving familiar faces, the tears fell and the hankies waved.

I eventually settled back into the airline seat to enjoy the beginning of our journey into the unknown. And what a bloody journey it was.

We were the last to stagger off the plane at Heathrow, having knocked back the G & T's in a rush when we heard the plane was landing sooner than we'd expected.

Inside Terminal One we secured a trolley, loaded the six pieces of hand-baggage and with the three kids still leaping with excitement, set off on a two-mile hike to Terminal 3. Here we would check in for the middle, and longest leg of our journey.

What with all the planning, confusion and excitement leading up to this point, it was only as we entered Terminal 3 that we realised Ziggy's new employers had chosen a Bank Holiday weekend for us to effect our migration. Heathrow airport was packed.

I found a relatively clear bit of space and settled down on the floor with the kids to read them a 'Mr Men' story whilst Ziggy went off to buy currency more appropriate to our destination.

I got three-quarters of the way through the exploits of Mr Small before discovering that I was reading to myself - and several bemused onlookers. The kids had buggered off to look for their Dad.

I rose nonchalantly to my feet, stacked our scattered possessions back onto the trolley and took it, and my red face, in search of my dear children.

Once re-assembled - easier said than done - we decided to get something to eat, so being the dutiful mother I spent ten minutes in the queue at the self-service cafeteria trying to buy some gold-plated (should have been at the price) sandwiches.

I returned to our table to find Brad at someone else's, helping himself to their chips, and the twins polishing off some Kit-Kats that some member of our family had managed to slip them when I wasn't looking.

Ziggy and I were just about to tuck into the sandwiches when we realised our flight was being called. Not to be caught out, we went straight through Passport Control and whilst I went to buy our Duty Free allowances, Ziggy and the children took a slow walk to Gate 47.

They must, however, have been calling our flight long before we first heard them because while deciding which perfume to buy I heard:

This is the final call for the one remaining passenger
on Flight QZ 003 to Lusaka.

Panic set in. I made hysterical screeching noises at the assistant to sell me whichever bottle of perfume she had in her hand and tore out of the shop clutching my plastic bags.

According to television programmes I had previously seen, most passengers using the moving pavements at large airports could be seen gliding sedately along the corridors holding polite conversation. I reckon the combined speed of me and that conveyor belt must have reached about forty-five miles an hour as I charged across what seemed like half of Greater London to reach Gate 47 and I certainly did not hold any conversations along the way.

I had never realised how many pairs of eyes you could fit into a Boeing 707, but I now know that it is an awful lot and they were all boring into me. Laden with my purchases, I lurched down the entire length of the plane to our second-from-the-back-row seats.

The ten hour flight to Lusaka was surprisingly calm, if you discount the chaos surrounding the installation of night-nappies and pyjamas in the confines of an aeroplane. The kids slept soundly from sheer exhaustion. Ziggy also slept soundly - but then he would after imbibing umpteen gin and tonics. I tossed and turned in my seat, wondering if we were right to be pursuing such an unusual course, though it was a bit late to be deliberating over that one, with us halfway to Africa and thirteen crates full of our possessions following behind on a paddle steamer.

I was just starting to doze off when some idiot switched the lights on and said it was time for breakfast. I thought my watch had stopped. It was only four o'clock!

Brad was the only one who woke up to have something to eat, whilst Ziggy and the twins slept on, oblivious to the chatter and clatter going on around them. After the breakfast trays had been cleared away I woke Vicki and Leon to get them dressed ready for our arrival in Lusaka. I'd finished Brad and Leon and had just started on Vicki when we had to buckle ourselves in. Just when I really didn't need it, they told us the flight was landing ahead of time.

We spilled off the plane to be greeted by a lovely warm, post-dawn breeze and strolled across the tarmac to the arrivals gate at Lusaka International Airport.

Apparently, I was not the only one surprised by the early arrival. Half of the airport staff hadn't turned up for work yet and the entire planeload of passengers had to wait squashed up in a corridor as the solitary cleaner finished hosing down (I kid you not) the Arrivals Hall.

Whilst Ziggy battled to find and complete the necessary paperwork and track down our luggage, I attempted to keep the rest of the family united with the hand baggage, at the same time as trying to finalise the dressing of Vicki. This was the cue for the next airport announcement asking the Patras family to urgently check in for the Kitwe flight.

2

Once more gathering our possessions, we moved through to Domestic Departures where we were told to board for the final airborne leg of our journey. By the time I'd packed everything back into the travel bag, we were last to embark yet again. Only this time it wasn't funny. The plane was chock-a-block full.

Ziggy set himself down in a seat halfway along the aircraft, with Brad on his lap. Only one seat remained right at the front, which had to accommodate myself plus Vicki and Leon. We were all supposed to have our own seats. What bothered me was that the seats our kids should have been occupying were filled by 'big people' and just about all of these big people had arrived on the same UK flight as us - complete with appropriate vast amounts of baggage. Surely the plane would be over its weight limit?

I buckled myself into the seat and held on to the two squirming bodies in my charge, for whom the novelty of going on planes had by now worn off. I felt much the same way myself. But none more so than when I peered between the bobbing heads and saw what lay before me.

The door which separated the cabin from the cockpit was swinging merrily on a hinge-and-a-half. Each time it swung open I could see this little Zambian chap trying desperately to cram dozens of enormous bulging suitcases into what looked like a gorilla cage behind the Captain's seat. And where the odd suitcase was small enough to slip out between the bars, he secured it in place by tying it up with a length of thick string. When he had eventually succeeded in his quest, he closed the aircraft door, pulled down a collapsible seat, donned a pair of headphones and sat beside the pilot, who was finalising his pre-flight check.

Shit, I thought, *this baggage handler is also the co-pilot!*

I had been travelling the skies since I was eleven years old and never once had I been scared. Now I was terrified. This rickety little flying machine, crammed to the gunwales with burly adults and their overweight luggage, was to be lifted into the air with the assistance of two pathetic looking prop-driven engines and a baggage handler!

I felt physically sick. No way was this plane going to get off the ground. As we taxied out to the very edge of the runway my insides felt like they were made of lead. The engines whined, the fuselage shook and the connecting door flapped back and forth on its wounded hinges. The plane bucked and rattled against its brakes until the Captain thought he had enough power for take-off.

Then we crawled forward.

Very, very slowly we trundled down the runway. Further and further we crept along. I felt sure the pilot would have to put on brakes, turn around and try again, when gradually my seat tipped back as the front end of this heap eased off the ground. We had lost sight of the terminal buildings long ago and were on the verge of ploughing the field of a neighbouring farm when the rest of the vibrating contraption became airborne.

Eventually the tension eased as it became apparent that we were actually going to stay in the air and the knots of leaden worms in my gut began to dissolve.

Next a tap on my shoulder announced the arrival of Brad who, clutching his paper bag and climbing onto my lap between Vicki and Leon, declared that he was going to be sick.

Never before had one small airline seat been occupied by so many.

I tried to turn around to indicate to Ziggy that he should fetch Brad, but it was impossible due to the fact that I still had my seatbelt fastened and was unable to unbuckle it because of all the children on top of me. And it was pointless trying to shout to Ziggy, as you couldn't hear a darned thing above the din of the engines.

Oh, what a memorable flight that was. If I live to be a hundred I know I shall never forget it.

After an hour, the plane touched down and we tumbled out with great relief into the hot dry air of Kitwe's Southdown Airfield. We looked around for a terminal building but all we could find was a corrugated tin hut, which turned out to be it.

The enthusiasm and anticipation that fired us prior to leaving England had now been replaced with apprehension and trepidation, just as England's green and lush fields had been replaced by the pale and arid land which lay before us. And we were questioning what the devil we had let ourselves in for.

A black face with a big smile and a placard reading "Rhinestone" stood beside a company bus which had been despatched to collect us and three other Rhinestone newcomer families from the 'airport'. Introducing himself as Wilkins, he greeted us all enthusiastically and after supervising the stowage of our baggage ushered us aboard comparatively luxurious transport. We settled back in our seats but everyone seemed rather shell-shocked by the preceding experience, so the atmosphere on the bus was somewhat subdued.

Then someone chirped up, "Well, what a flight that was" which snapped everyone out of their lethargy and in no time at all we were exchanging names, whilst kids were running up and down the bus from window to window.

"Wow, look at that tree, it's growing out of a sand-hill."

We were told by Wilkins that these were termite mounds, some of which could reach two or even three metres in height.

"Mummy, look at those funny houses," as we passed small round huts with mud walls and thatched roofs.

"Hey, look at those weird sheep – some of 'em's got horns!"voiced by a six-year-old belonging to a couple we were talking to. He had spotted a herd of goats.

It wasn't long before we saw signs of civilisation, as scruffy white buildings began to appear beside the road. As it widened, the street became lined with trees and houses, before progressing into shops and commercial looking buildings - some were even two stories high!

After negotiating two large roundabouts and a single set of traffic lights we found ourselves in the heart of Kitwe, the principal city of Zambia's Copperbelt Region. Our little bus drew to a halt outside the impressive multi-storey Edinburgh Hotel.

We were warmly welcomed by Doug, Ziggy's new boss, before checking in at the hotel. We were shown to our room. It had two single beds. When I enquired as to where the children were to sleep I was told that the hotel did not realise we had any.

We were passed through the hands of the entire Hotel Edinburgh Reception staff – from porter and various clerks before eventually getting the attention of a manager, to be told that we would be allocated a larger, or two adjoining rooms 'now'.

By the time negotiations had reached this level I was working solo, as Doug had carted Ziggy away for a briefing, so I decided I would take the kids for some fresh air and sunshine. That was until someone said such a course of action was not to be recommended. I was advised that in order to safeguard it from being stolen, I should stay with our luggage in the temporary room until I could accompany all our possessions to the new room, where it could then be safely left under lock and key.

This implication of lack of security did not sit well with my already strained nerves, nor did the prospect of spending any length of time cooped up in a hotel cell with three small, very bored children.

Although our three children had all been subjected to the same upbringing, I was (quite stupidly) surprised by the difference in their characters.

All three being premature, they had taken some time to catch up size-wise to other kids their age. However, size made no difference to their mental capacity.

Brad was talking quite early in comparison to the children I came in contact with at the various 'mother and child' appointments or activities. Despite being smaller than his playmates it soon became apparent that he was not going to be pushed around.

I won't bore you with the scores of misdemeanours the little sod accumulated during his first three years, other than to relate one tale of when he first attended playschool.

Vicki and Leon were about 5 months old and Brad was eligible to join a playgroup near to where we lived. It seemed like a good idea for him to spend time with kids his own age, so he attended three mornings a week.

One morning, a few weeks after he started there, I was 'summoned' by the head of the establishment.

"Mrs Patras, I'm afraid we have a slight problem with Brad. He has taken to hitting some of the other children."

Oh, no. Not my little angel.

"What happened?" I enquired.

"Well, it would appear that he just walks up, thumps a boy's arm and says, 'So there'."

I assured Mrs Thompson that I would address the situation with him and make sure that it did not happen again.

As I pushed Vicki and Leon in the Mighty Chrome Twin Pushchair up the long slog of a very steep road home, Brad displayed no signs of having done anything wrong.

After they had all been fed and watered I sat beside Brad at the table.

"So Brad Anthony, let's talk about what you have been doing at school today. The teacher told me you've been hitting some other children. Why did you do that?"

With a look which said he couldn't understand why this should be a problem, he said, "Well, they're all bigger than me, so I hit 'em back first!"

Needless to say, this practice was nipped in the bud very smartly.

We made a point of never referring to Vicki and Leon as 'the twins' as we felt they must be treated as separate individuals. However, for the efficiency of using two syllables instead of five when talking about them collectively, they were often referred to as 'the kids'.

As they reached the 'do something naughty' age, roughly when they turned one year old, Brad, at the grand old age of two-and-a-half, would come trotting along with a sneaky smile on his face.

"Mummy, have you seen what *those kids* are doing?"

By the time we moved to Zambia *those kids* were clearly developing their own personalities.

Leon James was the charmer, the chatterbox, the showman.

Victoria, the elder by five minutes, was a little quieter and, for the most part, more sensible. Naturally being one girl against two boys (and her mother's daughter) she learned to toughen up very quickly.

None of them lacked confidence, which came as no surprise given their parentage.

Over the years people have asked me, "Who is your favourite?"

FAVOURITE? What sort of a question is that?

"Well Brad of course," I said, "being my first born. And Victoria naturally, being my beautiful, only daughter. And Leon without a doubt, because he's my baby, my last born."

Favourites, indeed!

We were eventually released from the room after about an hour, shown our revised accommodation and were able to deposit our belongings, then lock up and go.

By this time I was seriously in need of a drink.

Accompanied by my little tribe, now armed with an assortment of toys

14

retrieved from a suitcase, we tracked down the Terrace Bar. I had experienced larger entertainment areas in my previous life but it was quite pleasant, if a little crowded, with three other families and four couples all enjoying suitable refreshments.

As the children entertained themselves I sat with a cold beer and mused.

I was quite surprised to see clouds. I don't know why I had not expected to see clouds, maybe it was because the Zambia Tourist Board brochure we had been sent said September would be dry and hot, and so I assumed that meant no clouds. Within a short time I was relieved that we *did* have clouds, as they gave welcome relief to the blazing heat of the sun. But they were really strange clouds.

These clouds were startlingly white against an azure sky and whilst the top and sides of the clouds looked all soft, fluffy and puffy, like a mountain of cotton wool balls or a child's drawing, the base of each cloud was completely flat, as though someone has sliced off their bottoms with a sharp knife, or as if they were sitting on a horizontal sheet of glass.

Despite the twelve kilometre drive into town from the airport I had not, until this point, noticed that the traffic was driving on the left. For some weird reason I had expected it to drive on the right - probably because we had crossed the English Channel. But when I considered it sensibly, it would be obvious to anyone with half a brain that vehicles would drive on the left, Zambia being an ex-British colony and all.

It soon became apparent that the toys my kids had brought along were quite a scarcity in this area and the majority of our time was spent trying to prevent the treasures being squirrelled away by other junior hands. Recognising that a revolt was imminent, I packed the toys away and decided to check out the local scene.

Having lived most of my life in an English town, my experience of cities was pretty limited, but what spread before me barely resembled my perception of the word 'city'.

We strolled into an open square about the size of a football field, which consisted of parking spaces surrounded by a couple of dozen shops. No bustling traffic and no busy office-wallahs scurrying around. In fact hardly any traffic and certainly no-one scurrying. But I was instantly overwhelmed when I saw the number of black people present.

Yes, I can hear you clearly.

"What the devil did you expect, you stupid woman? You're in the middle of Africa for God's sake!"

Well, I just hadn't thought about it that far, okay?

Whilst people went about whatever business, leisure or otherwise they were engaged in, I did not feel entirely at ease. Not that I was being threatened or anything. No-one was giving us the evil eye, there weren't hordes of men wearing leopard skins and brandishing spears closing in around us, or anything remotely menacing. I just felt so conspicuous, being white. Within ten minutes we returned to the hotel terrace where I felt more comfortable.

We were reunited with Ziggy shortly thereafter.

Later, after tea on the terrace and a quick bath, the kids were put to bed earlier than usual that evening and we left them safely tucked up in the knowledge that they would sleep soundly after the excitement of the past thirty-six hours. We went in search of a bite to eat in the hotel restaurant.

Ziggy chose to try a Zambian dish and asked the waiter for a recommendation. Apparently *nshima* and relish was the most popular. Being less adventurous in my eating habits I opted for steak and chips.

Cutlery already laid on the table was changed as appropriate and drinks were ordered. Whilst we waited for our meal to arrive Ziggy told me what he had learned from Doug during the course of his briefing.

He said that the following day, Sunday, Doug and his wife would collect us from the hotel to accompany us to our next level of accommodation. We wondered how many levels there were going to be. Was this some sort of test, or what? Or perhaps a traditional African custom in which we had to be initiated?

Before we could ponder this further, our food arrived. A huge piece of fillet steak filled my plate and looked delicious. Ziggy stared at his. It was a large plate with a mound of something on it that vaguely resembled mashed potato. Then a bowl was placed before him with a sort of gravy/sauce in it, which looked like it might contain some meat too. His hands reached either side of the plate for his knife and fork but the area was devoid of anything metallic, so he called for the waiter and pointed out this omission.

The waiter smiled benevolently.

"You see, sir, you do not eat it with the knife and the fork. You eat it with the fingers."

Ziggy looked from the plate of stiff white stuff, to the dish of brown sloppy stuff, to the smiling waiter and raised both eyebrows.

"Sir," said the waiter, suddenly producing a spoon, "may I?"

"Oh, please. Be my guest," replied Ziggy, gesturing with a wave of his hand towards the food.

The waiter then carefully took a spoonful of the white stuff and with a flourish transferred it to the palm of his left hand. He then discarded the spoon and with his right hand carefully pressed the knuckles of two fingers into the ball of goo to form a hollow. He then transferred this to his right hand, making sure that Ziggy was following every move carefully.

"Now sir, you take your *nshima* like so and..." the waiter made a swooping motion with his goo scoop above the sauce dish, "then take up the relish from the dish and, hey presto, you eat it. Lovely, sir."

On that happy note he disappeared with the spoon and his sample *nshima* scoop, leaving Ziggy in stunned silence.

It is not easy eating steak when you are trying with all your might not to laugh, which was made no easier when I glanced around and saw several bemused fellow diners observing this demonstration, also trying to suppress laughter behind politely raised hands or napkins.

But I had to hand it to Ziggy (if you'll pardon the pun). He did manage to

16

get about a third of the way through his 'traditional dish' before excusing himself to go and wash.

Upon his return he said, "That was quite nice actually."

I said nothing. I could not remember the last time I heard him tell such a bare-faced lie. He never tried *nshima* and relish again.

3

September 1980

Dear All,

Well, here's the latest update. Nancy, do you remember me telling you about Ronnie Slicer, the boss's wife who I spoke to on the phone a few weeks before we left? Well, I met her on Sunday and it turns out her name is Molly. I thought Ronnie was a funny name for a woman, it must have been a lousy telephone line.

Anyway, she and Doug (the boss) have arranged for us to stay in a 'leave house' until our freight arrives. Apparently it is customary for people to have other people staying in their homes when they go away on holiday. How weird is that?

Molly also gave me a guided tour of the shopping facilities here. Oh dear...

Over coffee in the hotel on Sunday morning, Molly and Doug explained what our 'next level' consisted of, and it was nowhere near as dramatic as it had originally sounded, though it still seemed very strange to me.

When we went on holiday in England we would just cancel the milk and newspaper, lock the doors and bugger off. But it wasn't for me to question the customs of people living in Africa.

It transpired that some friends of theirs had gone to a national park for eight weeks, which Molly said was very fortuitous as it meant we had the full use of their house whilst we were waiting for our 13 crates to arrive. The thought of actually living in someone else's house in their absence, especially someone I didn't even know, made me feel strangely uncomfortable. A bit like sitting on a warm toilet seat recently vacated by someone else's bottom, but worse.

However, when I considered the alternative of being stuck in the Edinburgh Hotel eating *nshima* and relish, living in someone else's house and sitting on their toilet seat sounded like a far superior option.

Outside the hotel, the kids and I piled into Molly's car whilst Ziggy followed in Doug's vehicle with all our baggage. After off-loading our gear, Doug took Ziggy to show him the site where he would be spending so much of his time over the next twenty-four months.

My initial impression of Molly was that she was quite an assertive person, though not domineering, and it didn't take me long to figure out that I would be relying upon her heavily for advice in the weeks to come. She promised to give me a guided tour of the shopping facilities in Kitwe on

Tuesday, but in the meantime had come armed with some provisions to keep us going.

She brought a cooked chicken, soap, flour, eggs, bread, vegetables and half a box of butter.

How jolly odd, I thought, or words to that effect. I liked butter as much as the next man, but twenty-four slabs?

It would appear that butter was one of the many things in short supply at the time, so when she had the opportunity to bulk-buy, she purchased extra in anticipation of our needs. She then went on to explain the golden rules to be followed when living in a leave house. The top of the list being that one could use any of the existing supplies, *so long as one was able to replace them*, which apparently was much easier said than done. She was very specific about one item.

"Whatever you do, DO NOT use the Bisto gravy powder. It's one of those things which people stock up with when they go on holiday to the UK or South Africa. We never see it in the shops here."

How was I supposed to make gravy without Bisto? I could see life was going to be tough in the tropics.

A couple of hours (and beers, I suspected) later, Ziggy was dropped off, and after Doug and Molly departed we sat down to compare notes and take stock of our surroundings and its contents.

One of the first things to come under discussion, apart from 24 packets of butter, was the dog. And when I say dog, I mean a DOG, although anyone could be excused for thinking she was a lion. Her name was Nina and she was the biggest Great Dane I had ever clapped eyes on.

Unfortunately Nina had been seriously ill with tick fever and consequently was as thin as a rake, with every bone protruding under her sand-coloured coat. One of our obligations to her owners was to try to build her back up to full size. Full size?

We were relieved to find that none of the children were afraid of her, despite never having come across such a large dog before, let alone sharing their home with one.

There was also a cat. Little more than a kitten really, called Utsi - a Siamese sort of thing which did not appear to object too much to being hauled around by its tail. Vicki took an instant liking to it and could be seen walking with it tucked under her arm. I tried my best to convince her it wasn't a good idea to clutch it by the neck, but at Vicki's age it was very much a case of in one ear and out the other. I just hoped that the message sunk in before Utsi was throttled to death.

Next on the list of 'info Molly had imparted' was that Sandy and Ronald came with the house. No, they were not goldfish. They were the cook/houseboy and the gardener.

Despite having been sort of forewarned, we got quite a shock the next morning. Ziggy had showered and dressed and gone through to the living area to make a cup of tea – and instead found the table fully-laden with a large pot of tea, slices of paw-paw, a rackful of toast, butter, some jam and a strange black man in white overalls wandering about.

Ziggy's first move was to dash back to the bedroom and make sure I didn't come sauntering through to the lounge half naked.

What Molly had failed to mention was that Sandy would arrive at 7 o'clock, let himself in and get breakfast ready. Actually, I said he was a cook/houseboy, but he was hardly a 'boy' - he must have been sixty if he was a day, and quite a short old man. In fact, one half of him was shorter than the other, because he had odd legs and had to wear a built-up shoe on one foot. He walked with a limp and had a round, jolly face.

The other half of the team, Ronald, was a pleasant lad of about 15 or 16, who kept the garden tidy and helped Sandy with floors and things. There was a building at the bottom of the garden known as a *kaya* which I was told means servants' quarters, but which in this instance was used by Rob Stevenson for his photography. However, whilst the owners were away Ronald stayed in it so that he would be around as a deterrent to would-be burglars, if we wanted to go out at weekends.

I was beginning to get a bit neurotic about the constant references to theft since our arrival. What sort of place was this? I believe I forgot to mention that Ziggy's employment package had also included the provision of a night guard for our new home. I had assumed this was a precaution against marauding lions and rampaging elephants. Obviously I was wrong. It was for protection from pilfering people.

In this instance I would have thought Nina would have been a sufficient deterrent to burglars as we were told that her reputation travelled before her. She would sink her teeth into any person with black skin (apart from Ronald and Sandy thankfully) who came within the confines of the garden, or even those who didn't if she could get out to them.

Anyway, back to Sandy. Leon, being deprived of the excessive attentions of his beloved Nannan Doris, took to Sandy immediately. And as was the norm for anyone over the age of thirty, the old man was thoroughly enchanted by our lisping little charmer. All three kids referred to Sandy as 'that man'.

At around half past eleven on that first day in the leave house I decided to do something with chips for lunch. Having prepared the spuds, I went and asked Sandy, who was hanging out the washing, where he kept oil or fat for cooking them in. He was most dismayed that I had made a start on lunch and insisted on taking over, so I told him what I had planned and left him to it.

At twelve-thirty Ziggy arrived home, so we seated the children around the table and sat back in amazement.

The table was fully-laden, including side plates, butter knives and napkins. Cups and saucers, milk and sugar were placed at the far end for post-lunch tea. Then in came Sandy bearing a large plate of chips, a platter of sliced corned-beef, and a dishful of hot baked beans. This was followed by a huge crusty loaf on the bread board, which was placed beside Ziggy waiting to be sliced. (The bread, not Ziggy.)

It was like being in our own personal hotel. As soon as we had finished eating, the table was cleared and Sandy set about washing the dishes. Of course, I would need to prepare the evening meal myself as Sandy finished work at 4.30. I immediately decided that our main meal of the day would always be at lunch time.

And to think I had originally tut-tutted at the idea of having house servants. SHAME ON ME.

▤ ▤ ▤

Tuesday was set aside for Molly to take me on a grand tour of the shopping facilities in Kitwe. It didn't take long. What a bloody place! Goodness knows how I was expected to provide meals. There weren't many shops, but what there were had the most incredible contents.

There were two large supermarkets and I use that term *very* loosely. Both Government owned, the stocks were almost identical to each other and consisted mainly of Jik bleach, Colgate toothpaste, toilet cleaner, Ajax floor cleaner, Vaseline Petroleum Jelly and baked beans. (Designed to make you clean, smooth and regular?) And let's not forget the corned beef and enamel mugs. And I mean there were rows and rows of each of these things. Like standard supermarket shelves, five high by ten feet long, just full of Vaseline Petroleum Jelly.

Against the far wall of the supermarket which went by the name of ZCBC was a bank of fridges, some working, some not. These contained the most gruesome looking 'fresh' chickens I had ever seen.

Almost wrapped in plastic bags, the chickens - none bigger than a large pigeon - looked as if they had been inhumanely killed by being battered to death with a lump hammer. The colour of them was a purplish yellow, tinged with orange at the extremities. And the STENCH... Oh, it permeated the entire store.

It was the sort of smell which would result from fridges/freezers being accidentally switched off and the 'meltings' being allowed to settle under the cabinets and not cleaned up for several months. An unnecessary situation one would have thought, considering the three hundred bottles of Ajax sitting on the shelves but a few yards away.

There were other shops besides the two government supermarkets. These sold, almost without exception, the most disgusting selection of crimplene clothes you could ever imagine. Crimplene dresses, crimplene trousers, crimplene t-shirts, crimplene knickers, together with the odd pair of plastic shoes and flannelette sheets. Who on earth would want flannelette sheets in that hot weather I did not know.

The exceptions were a couple of reasonably well-stocked hardware stores and a shop called Southern Cycles which, in the absence of any bicycles whatsoever, had taken to selling some vague brand of coffee, tea, hair brushes, the inevitable array of cleaning stuffs and puncture repair kits.

There was also a government distribution point selling milk where, I was assured, you could purchase milk, provided supplies were good and you were prepared to join the queue at dawn.

Vegetables were readily available at the fresh produce market which was situated some way from the main shopping facilities. This consisted of a large wooden, open barn-like building containing about eighty stalls, *all selling the same stuff.*

The range of produce was limited to say the least, though you were safe if you liked cabbages, green peppers and warty, stunted cucumbers. Things like leeks and cauliflower were apparently very seasonal and considered a rare treat.

The highlight of the vegetable market was the stall belonging to a little Polish man called Mr Smith (yeah, right) where Molly went to buy eggs and chickens which Mr Smith reared on his own farm and sold twice a week. From him, if he took a liking to you and for an above average price, you could buy a chicken which looked like a chicken in both size and colour, and eggs which were as fresh as any in Kitwe.

Molly kindly introduced me to him and after informing him that my husband had Polish ancestry I was guaranteed to be on his list of favoured customers.

Meat was more fickle. There weren't many butchers in Kitwe and for the time being they only sold beef because pork was apparently out of season and lamb was non-existent. Unfortunately one seldom knew which day these butchers would have any meat, so the purchase thereof was very much the luck of the draw.

There was a smattering of other vendors, such as a flower shop, government owned book store, two office stationery outlets, a furniture store, a fabric retailer (mostly crimplene) and several shops selling souvenirs of

Zambia (mostly copper). There was also Kitwe Electrical, whose electrical stock seemed to consist entirely of incredibly expensive light fittings.

Then there were banks, travel agents (I certainly understood the need to travel!), a building society and a couple of Bookies, though goodness knows what the punters gambled on - besides the availability of beef - because I was told there were no race courses operating in Zambia.

The alternative to city centre shopping was Parklands. Parklands was a residential area not far from the leave house and which also accommodated a row of half a dozen or so shops set back from the road close to a main traffic roundabout. These comprised two mini-supermarkets, one owned by a Greek, the other by an Indian, also a pharmacy, a butcher (joke), a seller of camping gas and yet another government book store. Apparently the Greek shop actually sold ham once a week, but I tried not to get too excited until I found out which day.

It seemed that one thing that *could* be guaranteed. Wherever you shopped there was a shortage of very basic commodities – salt, cooking oil, flour, sugar, soap, washing powder, shampoo, and toilet rolls – of which there seemed to be a dearth when we arrived.

I dared to ask about the possible purchase of beers, not having seen any on our travels and Molly explained that alcohol had to be bought from Bottle Stores and pointed out the one at Parklands. Rumour had it that lookouts were secretly posted by the expatriate community to check when the bottle stores received deliveries. As soon as word got out, people would rush along to the appropriate establishment and stock up. When I asked how much one had to pay for beers, Molly imparted that you couldn't buy them unless you had a case of empties to take back.

"So how much do I pay for a case of empties to start me off?" I enquired.

"Oh, they won't sell you empties. The empties are sent straight back to the brewery to be refilled."

When we were dropped off at home after that scintillating shopping experience, I took myself off to the toilet and sat quietly by myself. I cried - but not for too long.

I gave myself a stern dressing down.

"You are British, and made of strong stuff, so pull yourself together, woman."

I returned to the mayhem typical of three young children having been abandoned for five minutes and as I set about making some exciting tomato sandwiches for tea I wondered how I would break the news to Ziggy about the beers. *He's going to just love this one*, I thought.

After the kids had been put to bed that evening, Ziggy and I sat once more to compare notes. When I told him about the beer situation he surprised me by emitting a slow chuckle instead of the outpouring of curses I had anticipated.

"Now it all makes sense," he announced.

"What does?"

"For the life of me," he said, "I couldn't understand Doug's parting shot as we left the office today, that he would bring two empty crates of beer to work tomorrow. I thought it must be another one of those strange African customs we've been encountering."

Ziggy recounted his day. He was to be based at Head Office for the first two weeks whilst the site office was being suitably equipped. This office would be a bit more elaborate than the Portacabin huts he had been accustomed to using on sites in the UK. The site office consisted of a house which had been left standing at the perimeter of the ground cleared for the erection of the new Cobalt Processing Plant. Ziggy was to be Site Manager of this project.

Not having encountered it before, I enquired exactly what cobalt was. He explained that it is a chemical element by-product of copper mining and as a 'radio isotope' is used in various medical and industrial environs. To the man in the street it is probably more commonly known as a colourant of glass, ceramics, paints etc. And there were literally tons and tons of the stuff to be had around Kitwe, the ground being crammed full of copper and all.

I was quite impressed. Not only was I to become a lady of leisure, but I was getting educated in the process .

I then described my shopping experience with Molly and said that I felt she and Doug had been a teensy weensy bit off the mark when they had previously advised that 'certain things' were not available in Zambia.

I also pointed out that in order to be able to do shopping of any description, the one thing that was clearly a prerequisite to the exercise was transport. Funnily enough this subject had also been brought up by Doug. Ziggy was informed he would be given a driver, who could be made available to me whether it be for shopping or socialising purposes, when he wasn't needed by Ziggy.

We appreciated this was a very gracious offer, but being quite an independent person all my life, the prospect of having to rely on someone else to drive me around did not go down too well, but we agreed it would have to suffice for now.

Little did I realise at the time that this was but a blemish on the arse of an elephant compared to some of the delights that awaited us.

September 1980

Dear All,

Guess what I was introduced to today? Okay, I know you can't.

We were shown our new house and it more than makes up for the lack of decent shopping facilities.

The house is a sort of straight zig-zag shape. Or an elongated H with the top right arm and bottom left leg missing. This is extremely difficult to describe in words. I'll draw you a sketch.

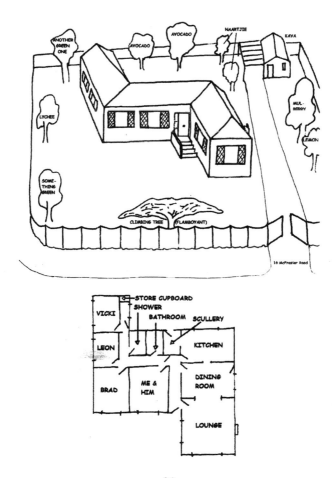

25

It is in Riverside, the same residential suburb as we are in at the moment, only about a mile further down the road and stands on a large corner plot bounded by a high, fancy concrete wall. It has a big garden with trees and stuff, most of which I have yet to identify.

Doug Slicer had imparted to Ziggy some time ago that he had found a nice, privately owned house available for the company to rent. It would seem these were not easy to come by as most housing was owned by the national mine, generally comprising pretty ordinary 3-bedroomed properties.

Apparently many people at Rhinestone wanted this house, but Doug insisted on keeping it for us, knowing that we would need four bedrooms. I was so delighted that Doug stuck to his guns.

As we walked around, the kids didn't know where to look first. They could not decide if it was more fun climbing inside all the cupboards and wardrobes, or tearing through the enormous garden. There was much excitement.

We had entered through the door at the rear of the property which led immediately into a small scullery area before opening out to the kitchen. The kitchen was lovely and big; a great relief as I had always been used to large kitchens in my previous life. Moving from the kitchen, we entered a passage which led to the dining room and lounge. These two rooms were separated by wooden fold-back doors which, when opened, made the area look even larger than it already was. There was a feature fireplace in the lounge which surprised me as I had been told that it never got cold in Zambia.

The plastered walls were painted white and the lounge and dining room both had parquet flooring, whilst the rest of the house was linoleum tiled.

After passing through a doorway from the 'living area' a long corridor led to the bedrooms and bathrooms.

From the wardrobe allowance it was obvious that the first one we encountered was the 'master bedroom', the next one along wasn't much smaller and would easily accommodate a single bed and leave enough space for a disco. On the other side of this corridor were the two bathrooms, one with a large bath, the other with a shower.

We then turned a corner to find two smaller bedrooms, both of which were larger than the average 'double bedroom' in a typical English house.

At the end of that passage was a fitted cupboard which later proved to be essential for storing all sorts of stuff one needed to 'buy in bulk when available'. On top of that, all of the bedrooms had oodles of fitted wardrobe space.

When it came down to bedroom allocation, I agreed to let Brad have the bedroom nearest to us, since he was more likely to wander out of his room at night, and being scared of the dark would make a fuss about being tucked away around the corner. Vicki, being the most fearless of the brood, copped for the room furthest away.

After a good squizz around we reluctantly left our future new home.

"It IS a big house, isn't it Mummy?" Vicki remarked.

Within half an hour of returning to our temporary residence, Brad asked, "Mummy, when can we go to The Big House again?"

Thus our future home had been named.

Our first week in deepest Africa was completed and we were all still in one piece. No-one had been bitten by a snake or eaten by a lion, though we were not exactly devoid of wildlife.

I suffer from arachnophobia. During one of my meetings with Molly, I had interrogated her on the subject of dangerous spiders and was told that she had never come across any.

She said that one sometimes found small 'jumping spiders' which, if one gave you a nip, could produce a sore little lump for a day or two. Other than those she had only ever seen 'wall spiders', whereupon she went in search of a wall spider, eventually tracking one down behind a mirror. As soon as she moved the mirror the spider shot out and dashed across the wall.

I dashed to the other side of the room.

When the spider was on the run, it moved like any other spider, body in the air, legs pointing in all directions travelling at 90 mph. But as soon as it stopped, it flattened its legs and body against the wall, looking almost as if it had been splattered, which I personally felt it should be. Only when disturbed does it hoist itself up on tiptoe again and hare off in its chosen direction.

Molly assured me that they were perfectly harmless and considered a desirable asset to any household because they eat mosquitoes which are much more of a hazard, being the carriers of malaria.

Then I was distracted by a lizard traversing the wall. I watched it with fascination for some time. Molly had said that they also were considered good to have around, as they too eat insects - and spiders if they became too plentiful. The lizards definitely got my vote.

Harmless or not I was certainly not enthralled when the next evening I spotted a big wall spider on the ceiling right above our bed. Enough was enough, so in the absence of any obliging lizard (like policemen, never around when you want one) I instructed Ziggy to get rid of it.

It wasn't enormous, but it probably measured over two inches across, legs included, which is far more than I can cope with. Ziggy scoffed at my refusal to deal with it and went to fetch the sweeping brush.

Armed with his implement and wearing only his underpants, he climbed onto the bed, where he tried to get a firm stand before making his assault. With the spider some two feet to his fore, and the brush some twelve inches from the ceiling, he jabbed at it, twisting his bristles.

I ran for the door, lest I should get leapt on (by the spider, not Ziggy) and looked over to where the action was, or should have been. In his haste not to have the spider fall onto *him*, Ziggy had sidestepped and fallen off the edge of the bed and was now picking himself up and dusting himself down. The spider was still on the ceiling. I was in a crumpled heap on the floor trying, unsuccessfully, not to laugh.

Ziggy climbed back onto the bed and proceeded to chase the spider across the ceiling. If a tarantula had dropped on me then I couldn't have done a thing about it. I simply could not move as I was bent over double, clutching my aching stomach from so much laughter.

I eventually looked up through streaming eyes when I heard a cry of "Gotcha, ya little bugger", and found Ziggy peering at the mutilated spider stuck to the end of his implement (the brush).

Needless to say he was not very impressed with my (un)supportive role during this skirmish and marched off with his booty.

"Next time you can kill your own bloody spiders."

I just nodded. I couldn't do much else. Every time I thought I had myself under control, I recalled the vivid picture of Ziggy bouncing about on the bed in his knickers, clutching his broom-stick and I just curled up again.

On the subject of the bed, that one in the Little House was the most uncomfortable piece of furniture I have ever had the misfortune to (try to) sleep on and I've slept on camp-beds, settees, train seats, plane seats, hammocks and floors.

It consisted of a metal frame with an old-fashioned set of coiled springs pointing towards the floor. On top of this sprung base was a solid sheet of plywood, as solid as plywood ever can be. This 'topcoat' thus made the springs beneath completely redundant.

Their only purpose, as far as I could work out, was to provide a sturdy place on which to bash your shins if you should be so ill-advised as to walk about the bedroom in the dark.

Over the plywood lay a piece of foam which, at a rough guess, started out about six inches thick but was now compressed into an assortment of odd-shaped hollows ranging from two to five inches deep. I could only wonder at the shape of the slumbering people who had managed to contort the foam into such a random mishmash of dents.

The pillows were something else. It was like resting your head on a sack of hard-boiled eggs with the shells still on – not that I have ever tried that, but I do have quite a fertile imagination.

I certainly would not be sorry to see the back of that setup when we moved to The Big House.

September 1980

Dear All,

Stop the bulk orders, cancel all shipments, the panic is over. No, I haven't found a toilet roll tree, but I have found an acceptable substitute. Paper serviettes.

I discovered them surreptitiously sitting on a shelf in the pharmacy in town, so I bought up as many packets as I could afford at the time and cut them into appropriate sized sheets which are now stacked on the back on the toilet cistern. Much better than having the Times of Zambia imprinted on your backside every day, especially as I have been told that if you are discovered 'defacing' our honourable President during such an act, you can be arrested.

This worries me somewhat. How would anyone get to know exactly what section of a newspaper I used to wipe my backside with in the first place? I have been searching for hidden cameras in our house but nothing has yet come to light.

Yesterday I did the unthinkable. Five minutes to seven in the morning, I was sitting on the loo, minding my own business, when Ziggy poked his head around the door and said, dead romantic like, "Happy Anniversary, Darling."

I had actually forgotten our wedding anniversary!

Mr Smart-Alec had to walk around with a smug 'who remembered and who forgot, then?' look on his face for the next hour. I am sure I will not be allowed to live this down for a long time. The best of it is, I actually remembered to buy him a card before we left the UK, but it's in the damned freight, isn't it?

Ahh, the wanderer has returned from work, or to be more accurate, from his first after-work 'quick-drink-but-it-turned-into-a-piss-up' session.

I'm sure you must admit, that we've rarely seen Ziggy drunk, but he is getting his 'worms' all mixed up and walking into the furniture. He swears it will be the last time he drinks that much, because he frightened himself silly driving home (you know how strict he is about not drinking and driving). Anyway, he seems very repentant and it is perhaps as well he's had that fling, so it puts him straight at an early stage.

To be fair he does have a pretty good reason for being out so long, as he had to go to a new members' meeting of the Nkana Kitwe Arts Society, in order for us to join.

This is the local 'Little Theatre' where they put on amateur productions roughly once a month.

That sounds bad. I don't mean they put on amateur productions roughly, I mean they occur approximately once a month. Well, they may do them roughly for all I know, considering we have not been to see one yet.

Having been forgiven my 'oversight' at forgetting our wedding anniversary, Ziggy offered to take me out for a meal that evening, so we called on Ronald to babysit and off we went to paint the town red. It would probably have been a damn sight easier to physically do that rather than try to find somewhere to celebrate, because we soon discovered that every restaurant in town was shut on a Monday night.

We did not fancy the rather limited cuisine of the Edinburgh Hotel, so instead decided to find a watering hole.

This was when the seriousness of a situation we had been told about actually hit home. There were no pubs. I heard the cry from afar. How could we, of all people, move to a country which had NO PUBS?

Well, no pubs as we knew them anyway. Apparently there were taverns to be found in the townships, but we were told they were not for the likes of us.

We were advised that people socialise at sports clubs, but we had not realised that it was the only option. This accounted for another of those 'odd things' we had found in our Contract - that Rhinestone would pay the annual subscription for membership of two sports clubs of our choice. That was all very well and good, but we were not 'sporty' people so had no idea what sports club we should join.

We discovered there were plenty of sports to choose from. Cricket, bowls, rugby, squash, golf, tennis, rowing, and many more, but we didn't hear of anywhere where they just played dominos, darts and cribbage, and drink beer, which were the 'sports' we were used to playing in the Burton Arms.

The previous weekend we had gone to the Kitwe Little Theatre with a few other Rhinestone employees to watch a film on elephant poaching, so we knew where the place was and that it had a bar, so decided to try our luck there.

Upon arrival, we were told it was strictly 'members only', but when we explained that it was our 6th Wedding Anniversary and we had nowhere to go to celebrate, one of the members took pity on us and signed us in as his guests.

We had a thoroughly enjoyable evening. There were not many people in the place but those present seemed friendly and the booze was cheap. We also noticed that it had a nice play area for kids and a rather superb swimming pool, *for use by members only,* so we found out more about joining the club. There were, however, a few draw-backs.

The theatre club only granted a three month provisional membership initially, during which time you had to 'prove yourself' by participating in club activities before being granted full membership.

I quite pictured myself as Lady Macbeth, wringing my hands and crying, "out damned spot." I'd done enough washing in my time so I figured I should be good at that. But I didn't much fancy Ziggy as Richard the Third, he never was very good with horses.

Fortunately participation also included helping make the scenery, which was right up Ziggy's street given his D.I.Y. expertise around our first home, or assisting in the wardrobe department, which fit nicely along my avenue of sewing experience.

We said that we would love to join and agreed that Ziggy would attend the New Members' Meeting the next day.

All told, our 6th Anniversary turned out to be a very pleasant and worthwhile night out. Well, that's what I thought at the time. If only I could have seen into the future.

We soon found ourselves spending a lot of time at the Little Theatre. We went along two weekends after joining and found out that the production currently in the pipeline was the Olde Time Music Hall. Apparently, they put one of these on every October and it was one of the most popular shows of the year. I managed to track down the woman who was in charge of the wardrobe and enquired what I could do to help.

She said that she had bought some fabric for the girls in the chorus line, so they could make up their skirts. She asked me if I would cut it into the appropriate lengths and be on hand to dish them out to the relevant people when they came along. That sounded simple enough.

She also said that some folk would want to get into the wardrobe to get hold of other costumes and gave me a key.

I never saw or heard from her again.

From what I gathered from some of the other members, she had been waiting for ages for some muggins to come along so she could hand over the wardrobe keys, and knowing no better I fell very nicely into the 'idiot' slot.

I soon had to be in attendance several nights to allow people access to the costumes. There seemed to be hundreds of people involved, most of whom were no more familiar with the contents of the wardrobe than I was.

I keep saying 'the wardrobe'. It conjures up pictures of dozens of people trying to cram themselves into a large wooden cabinet. Like – how many adults can you fit inside a telephone booth?

Actually, it consisted of a backstage room, about 8 x 4 metres in size, lined from floor to ceiling with shelves, which were crammed full with cardboard boxes bursting forth every variety of apparel you could possibly conceive - and some you couldn't. There were also a number of hanging rails in the centre of the room which any high street dress shop would be proud of.

People kept coming and asking me for things that, not only did I not know where to find, but I didn't even know what they were. For instance I had absolutely no idea what a morion was.

Every item removed from the wardrobe had to be written down in The Book and signed for. One Saturday, I got some very weird looks from people when I asked one rather good-looking chap what his name was, and then how to spell it, before I would let him remove a bowler hat. It appeared he was the *S*T*A*R* in a recent production of Jesus Christ Superstar, which had been such a hit that it was extended for two more weeks. But that was before my time, so how the devil was I supposed to know who he was?

Then I caught sight of one of the rehearsals and it really did look as if it was going to be very good.

(In case your curiosity is uncontrollably aroused … it would appear that a morion is a hat. More specifically one of those hats which looks like a black pith-helmet with a cock's comb running down the centre. But you already knew exactly what it was, didn't you?)

An old hobby I rediscovered was badminton. On a Wednesday night, Ziggy would sit at home whilst I went off to the local convent for a game of badminton. No, I wasn't playing against a load of nuns, the group consisted mostly of expat ladies and older men, none of whom were quite county league level so I wasn't too out of my depth.

Unfortunately, whilst enjoying this I missed out on watching some classic entertainment on the local television station. It seemed that quite a few people on Zambia Television could have taken tips from the Kitwe Little Theatre amateur players.

Ziggy told me about an unusual cookery program he watched during my absence. It would appear that the whole program was something of a joke, although it wasn't meant to be funny and Ziggy reckoned the 'studio kitchen' was the last word.

He said he could not remember what the woman was supposed to be cooking one particular night, but the recipe included onions. There was none of this 'here are some I prepared earlier' stuff which we had become used to on British cookery programs at in those days. She had to chop up her onions in full view of her audience.

The average Zambian housewife had very little in the way of modern equipment or gadgetry in her kitchen, but this woman had obviously recently acquired a Chopamatic, and was determined to show off to her public.

You are probably familiar with the Chopomatic. It looks like a large inverted plastic tub with a squiggly blade inside. When one punches the knob on top, the blade goes up and down and, hey presto, cuts through whatever has been placed under the tub, if you're lucky.

Apparently when this woman tried to chop her onion, instead of using a chopping board she placed a whole onion in a medium-sized Pyrex bowl, covered the onion with the Chopamatic and then proceeded to punch the said knob.

Of course, the bowl having a concave base prevented the blade from cutting all the way through the onion, so the onion naturally got impaled on the blade. As she frantically punched the knob, so the onion kept bobbing up and down inside the gadget, as whole and unchopped as the day it came out of the ground.

After a whole minute of abortive Chopamaticing, she upended the device, prised the onion off the squiggly blade and cut it up with a knife, saying not a blind word about the incident, as if this was all part of the process.

Ziggy confessed he didn't know what she then did with her onion, because he was laughing so much that his eyes were streaming tears and he missed the remainder of the show.

I asked the badminton club if they could meet on a different night, as this show sounded just too good to miss. Unfortunately my pleas fell on deaf ears.

October 1980

Dear All,

The bloody freight still hasn't arrived. I'm beginning to think that they really have sent it on a paddle-steamer. I'm a bit p...'d off about it actually because, as you know, it's Brad's 4th birthday on Thursday and all his presents and cards are in the crates. Fortunately at his young and tender age he won't notice if it's a few days (or weeks!) late, so we are simply not going to tell him that it's his birthday, and certainly make no mention of an overdue party. What awful parents we are.

I had a riotous time this afternoon - spent 35 minutes queuing outside a shop to buy Oxo stock cubes and salad cream! Don't anyone ever complain to me about the wait at Sainsbury's check-outs again. Nor about the price of Oxos .

I've been told that you virtually never see Oxo cubes in Zambia, so I bought 38 packets. Plus twenty packets of chicken stock cubes, four jars of salad cream, three drums of salt and two tubs of Bisto. All this came about because a new shop opened up in town and as a draw card they had imported, at great expense, assorted attractive items from South Africa. The only trouble is they sold out of everything (other than Vaseline, corned beef and Ajax) within an hour and a half of opening their doors .

I never thought I could get so excited about Oxos, but it's amazing what you do when you're desperate.

During the past week I have also acquired 40lbs of sugar, 24lbs of rice, 12lbs of cake flour (plain flour to you) and two separate half-boxes of butter. All of which, apart from the sugar, have to be stored in the deep freeze because of weevils (and going runny).

I didn't tell you about the weevils yet, did I?

Whilst I was not normally in the habit of ferreting around in other peoples' drawers - I was actually looking for scissors - I came across a gem of a publication in the sideboard at the Little House. It consisted of 30+ typed pages and was called 'Welcome to Kitwe'. It was full of information about (would you believe) Kitwe and life in Zambia generally.

It covered a multitude of subjects like where to go to eat out (though it said nothing about everywhere being closed on a Monday), useful phone numbers, nearby places of interest, information on local fruits and vegetables, etc.

The following extract intrigued me:

Fresh or dried Kapenta
Small fish which can be cooked like whitebait. The dried variety is more of an acquired taste. So are caterpillars and flying ants which you may well see on sale in the streets.

'URRGH'. However, with our current meat situation, I did not know what we may need to resort to.

There was also a section on photography, where one was warned that it could be hazardous to photograph certain everyday objects like bridges, post offices, airports and fire stations. You could be arrested for it.

We were also advised not to photograph:
• Police Officers on duty
• Road accidents
• Customs Halls and Officials
• 'Instant Justice' groups in the street

A paragraph contained under a section called 'Helpful Hints' also caught my attention.

It is not necessary to discard flour which is 'ropey' or flour, rice, nuts, etc, which contain small black weevils. These pests develop rapidly in the tropics and are harmless.
Sieve the flour; wash rice, nuts, etc., as weevils float to the surface and can be poured off.

I suddenly went off beef curry and rice. Though thinking about it, if I couldn't get beef and didn't bother to wash the rice... No, perhaps not.

But by far and away the best entry in this reference of riveting reading related to the putzi fly, on which I gleaned more information.

It would appear that the putzi fly harbours a fascination for wet washing. In order to reproduce, it lays its eggs in wet or damp areas of clothing or linen, notably in slower-drying areas such as seams or hems. When the clothing is later donned by some innocent primate, the eggs hatch and creep out from the cloth and burrow under the skin. The grubs grow fat and wriggly and cause septic sores, which one should not scratch or squeeze.

'Treatment should be administered by applying a thick blob of Vaseline to the affected area'.

So that's why there was so much Vaseline around!

The fat, wriggly grub, deprived of its immediate source of oxygen through the skin, squiggles to the surface until its ugly little head pops out. The fat wriggly grub can be squoze (is there such a word?) out and deposited down the nearest toilet. It is advisable to wash out the resulting pit (in the skin) with some sort of antiseptic solution.

Alternatively you could kill the little buggers off first by ensuring that ALL clothes, sheets, towels, etc are thoroughly ironed before being worn or used, as the excessive heat destroys the eggs.

I noticed that there was no mention of all THAT in the *What You Need To Know About Zambia* booklet posted to us in the UK by the Zambia Tourist

Information Board.

After reading the recently discovered pages, you certainly were *Welcome to Kitwe* as far as I was concerned.

My original determination not to cow-tow to the colonial habit of hiring house-servants had long been abandoned, especially having discovered the need to iron bed-sheets and towels, as well as every single item of clothing, socks and underwear included.

I discussed with Molly the issue of hiring a houseboy for the Big House. It appeared great care had to be taken when appointing the services of a house servant, as many of them were inclined to have sticky fingers.

Molly put me on to a chap who was a cousin of her house-servant Austin and we were promised that if he stepped out of line Austin would 'get him'.

His name was Foster and he had a face the likes of which I had never seen in my life. He had only one eye and half his teeth. Well, that is not strictly accurate.

He did not just have one eye and an empty socket. He had two eyes, one which worked and one which did not and the one which didn't was usually pointing up into his skull so all you saw of it was a huge white blob.

Occasionally it slipped round to the front and looked almost normal, which was even worse, because then I could not remember which eye to look at when I spoke to him. I always look people in the eye, well, usually *eyes*, when I speak to them.

As far as his teeth were concerned, he appeared to have neither quantity nor quality. He only had one front top tooth, which more than made up for the lack of the others, in so far as the one he had was HUGE. It stuck out at an angle and protruded over his lower lip. He had two or three other top teeth of assorted shapes and sizes on the right side of his mouth, but not a single one on the left.

I was not sure about his bottom teeth, I did not bother to pursue the issue that far. All I knew was that the combination of what he had and did not have, resulted in his mouth taking on such a distorted twist that, together with the lisp caused by the lack of teeth, I could hardly understand a bloody word he said, even when he managed to speak in what I presumed was English.

Still, I was told he was good at polishing floors, so we hired him.

It is the norm for house servants to live in the *kaya*, as most come from villages which can be many miles away and only return to their home on their days off, or even less regularly depending on the distance involved. Being unused to servants, or total strangers living on our property, we were not really keen on the idea of Foster 'living in'. However, his plight was punted by a friend. Apparently Foster's two eldest children needed to attend school, and as there wasn't a government school in his village, he wanted to have them live with him in the *kaya* so they could go to their local school in Kitwe. We found it difficult to turn down such a plea so agreed to the arrangement.

We had been told by Molly that the servants kept quietly to their own quarters and were self-sufficient, other than being provided with a regular supply of mealie meal –powdered maize which *nshima* is made from and which forms the major part of their staple diet. There were also a few other little perks which would be expected once we took up residence in the Big House.

In the meantime we had a wonderfully clean, empty property which we could not live in.

A typical day at this point in our lives started at about 6.15 when our neighbour's houseboy arrived whilst they were obviously still sleeping. Armed with a half brick he would proceed to rap loudly on the iron gatepost, until his employer deigned to shift his arse and let him in. I seriously considered letting Nina out to encourage him to gain entry *over* the gate, because this little ritual invariably woke our three cherubs much more rapidly than he woke his employer.

Once awakened, Ziggy would disappear to the bathroom and leave me to endure the, "I want a cup of tea" and "I've done a poo, Mummy" routine from the kids, whereafter they exited, leaving me to drift back off to sleep for five more precious minutes amidst the acrid smell of discarded nappies.

By the time I arose, the children had just about emptied all their drawers trying to decide what not to wear today and I would slip quietly off to the bathroom, hopefully unnoticed.

We would eventually settle down to breakfast, which was an excitement as we tried to guess which way the eggs would be presented. Would they be boiled, fried, poached, scrambled or omeletted? Breakfast over (not as easily done as said) and on to the task of removing the egg from chins and tummies.

Next, each child would present his or her choice of clothes for the day, ie. green shorts, orange t-shirt and blue socks, for my assistance with dressing, which would then be followed by 'hunt the shoes'.

Having eventually shoved the children outside to play I was then faced with the dog. Nina would stand by the front door and growl at me until I went outside to participate in a five minute wrestling ritual with her, until I staggered back indoors to return once more to the bathroom, this time to rid myself of the blood, slobber and dog hairs.

The morning would continue fairly quietly with whatever I was doing continually interrupted by kids wanting pop, biscuits, bananas, stories or the paddling pool re-filled. By 11.30 I usually realised that I had forgotten to put beers in the fridge to cool and as they had been standing in the full sun all morning I would resort to giving a few bottles a quick drenching under the cold tap before putting them into the freezer to quick-chill.

At one o'clock or thereabouts the lord and master arrived home for his lunch. At 1.30 he would return to work. It was then time for the children to take a nap. Unfortunately Brad would only have a nap if I did, so that meant that all four of us were 'out' for an hour or so, depending on how hot it was.

Nearing five o'clock in the afternoon was the time to see the local women returning home from their vigil outside the shops.

Each would be wearing a brightly-patterned piece of cotton material called *chitenge*, which formed a wrap-around skirt over their normal clothes. Tied at the waist the *chitenge* reached almost to the floor. The fabric would have a recurring theme every 18 inches or so – some of these fabrics even sported head and shoulders pictures of President Kaunda. Actually, I was surprised that they could get away with that, given that when they sat down they would be sitting on the president's face!

Droves of women congregated in town each day and just sat around on the pavements outside the main supermarkets on the off-chance that some essential commodity might be delivered, returning home (wherever that might be) before dusk, usually carrying goodness knows what inside a bag, a sack or a huge enamel washing-up bowl, which they balanced competently on their heads.

Virtually every one of the women also sported a baby strapped to her back with a shawl, towel or narrow piece of fabric. Whilst you seldom saw a woman without a baby, you rarely saw any toddlers or young children by her side. I could not think where they stashed them. I figured perhaps there had been a ban on having kids and they had only just started breeding again in the past year or so. I later discovered that they left them 'at home' with members of their extended families – grannies, sisters, aunties, cousins, etc., but initially I had absolutely no idea about those things.

Shortly after the exodus of women, came the labour force being driven home.

Hundreds of men were crammed in the back of lorries, which came in a multitude of shapes and sizes. But they didn't just stand up in the trucks, they also sat on the roof of the cab, or on the rear and side panels, with their arses hanging over the edge. The state of some of the roads in Kitwe left a lot to be desired and as the vehicles bounced in and out of the potholes it was a miracle that the passengers all stayed in, or on, at all.

One of the other great mysteries was the shape of the trucks and buses. I came to the conclusion that they must buy them from a specialist manufacturer, as they all had the same trait – lopsided bodies and back wheels which took a different route to the front wheels. They looked like they were driving crab-wise. No wonder so many ended up in ditches.

7

October 1980
Dear All,
Yippee, hurray, hallelujah, whoopee, the ecstasy, the
heavenly sounds that caress my ears, the sheer joy of
once more using my typewriter. You will never understand
the relief felt by my poor aching knuckles on being able
to release the vice-like grip on a ball-point pen and
return to the familiar, fast-reacting tapping of the
keyboard. May biros be banished from the letter-writing
side of my life for ever.
Yes, you guessed it, the freight has arrived. The first
thing on my list to be unpacked was, naturally, the
typewriter. The trouble I have writing by hand is that my
pen can't keep up with me and I finish up missing out
half of the words. I know some of my letters don't make
much sense at the best of times, but with so many words
missing, they must become even more of an enigma.

The first two days after the grand arrival were spent wading through the crates. It seemed such a long time since we crammed all our worldly goods into those boxes that I had forgotten just what I had packed and was very pleasantly surprised when I found out.

Naturally we had the crates delivered straight to the Big House. It was like Christmas and everyone's birthday rolled into one. Brad got so excited, he wanted to unpack all of them on the first day, but I needed to be very careful about what boxes I opened in front of him. I did not want him catching sight of any of the presents we had brought out. Meanwhile, Vicki and Leon spent their time playing hide and seek around the crates.

The only disappointment was that whilst all our stuff was now safely ensconced in our own house, we were hardly able to use any of it, as we were committed to remain at the Little House until the rightful occupants returned from leave at the end of the month.

Another upside with the arrival of the crates was that we could now permit Brad to be four years old. It didn't take long to track down his first 2-wheeler bike, though locating the birthday cards took more effort.

We organised his birthday party for two days later, though to describe it as a party is a gross exaggeration, since there were only four guests and one of those was another child's mother. It is not that we were being frugal, we just didn't know many people with children at the time.

The fare for the occasion was pathetic and consisted mostly of corned beef sandwiches, tomatoes and hard boiled eggs, so I was greatly relieved at being able to adorn what passed for a birthday cake with the little coloured candles I had put in one of the crates, a true luxury as we were told the only candles available in Zambia were the big white ones we used when there was a power cut.

Even making the birthday cake was quite a mission because one could only buy bog-standard sugar (if you were lucky), never caster sugar, or icing sugar. So before making the cake I had to 'make' the sugar, by putting granulated sugar in the liquidiser of my little Kenwood and whiz it until it became finer. For icing sugar, one just whizzed a lot longer, resulting in all kitchen surfaces within a six-foot vicinity being coated in white sugar-dust.

Brad was thrilled with his bicycle and enjoyed falling off it constantly for the first week. We had also taken a few extra gifts for Vicki and Leon so they wouldn't feel left out. A few days later I was concerned by the lack of noise surrounding the kids and went to investigate. Walking outside I found three budding Jack Nicklaus's, with intense concentration furiously failing to hit giant sized plastic red golf balls with jumbo plastic golf clubs.

But what made the sunny picture so classic was the fact that their golfing attire, to a man, consisted solely of a pair of red towelling knickers and red wellington boots. Now if Jack Nicklaus had followed that trend, golfing might have had a totally different appeal.

As well as the birthday things and other wondrous stuff I then had access to, I was very relieved to find the swimming armbands. I had not realised just how essential they were until one day when I was playing with the kids on the steps of the pool at the theatre.

Leon was waist deep on the broad second step and tried to reach a ball which was floating on the surface but overbalanced and fell forward. Instead of righting himself, he floated, face down on the top of the water. Of course I reached out and retrieved him immediately, but it was very scary the way he just floated there, instead of trying to put his feet down to stand up. This close call warned me to keep a very close eye on all of the children even when they were only paddling on the steps.

Kitwe, the second largest city in the country, was the hub of the Copperbelt in the sort-of-north of Zambia. Actually, it's nowhere near as far north as you can go, because Zambia is a peculiar shape, a bit foetal, the most northerly region being on the eastern side of Zambia, where nothing much seemed to be going on from what I could gather. It would appear that the only thing really worth bothering about in the eastern 'blob' was Luangwa National Park, which covered a huge area and was full of wild things African.

Kitwe itself bore little resemblance to any English city I had ever visited. The city centre - you know, shops, offices and the like, more resembled a very small English town centre. If you stood in the dead centre (middle of the city, not in the cemetery), the commercial sector could probably have been covered by walking no more than 300 metres in any given direction.

There was not much in the way of designated car parks, but the wide streets provided adequate kerbside parking for those lucky enough to have cars.

The roads in the city centre were in slightly better condition than those outside town mainly because they didn't get fast moving, heavy traffic. Some of the pavements were quite rough, with missing or grossly cracked and uneven paving slabs. And whilst there wasn't a lot of litter around, there was a strangely grubby feeling to the place.

Upon leaving the city centre the streets were lined with houses even before you reached the defined residential suburbs, which made up the greater areas of Kitwe.

Generally speaking, houses were detached and quite spacious. You wouldn't see terraced houses and there were very few semi-detached properties. Ninety-five per cent were single storey structures standing in large gardens and usually surrounded by six-foot high walls or wire mesh fences. Many (unfortunately not ours) had swimming pools.

They were all brick built (not mud and thatch) and most had tiled roofs, except for a lot of the mine-owned houses, many of which had corrugated roofs which were often painted blue, pale green or a terracotta red. These tended to be smaller dwellings.

And there were lots and lots of trees. This wasn't immediately obvious until you came to stand on higher ground and attempted to spot the houses which you would think, given their size, would be quite easy to spot. Actually, standing on higher ground was not that simple, as Kitwe is very flat. My only experience of looking down on it was from the 5th floor bedroom window of the Hotel Edinburgh.

Once out of the centre it was rather like living out in the country, in that there were no pavements to the tarred roads. Most of the roadsides had storm drainage ditches, sometimes three to four feet wide and at least as deep, depending on the terrain. Locally known as *dongas*, these were either right next to the road or set back a few feet, leaving room to walk between the ditch and the tarmac, if you were lucky.

Not long after we arrived, we were driving down a road when we saw an enormous blue tree. I could not figure it out. There was not a sign of green on it, just a blue form stretching high into the azure sky.

We soon discovered it was a jacaranda in full bloom and it was incredibly beautiful. Another tree coming into flower at the time was a flame-red/orange one with bright green, fern-like leaves and enormous seed pods hanging down. These resembled gigantic runner beans, some of which were green but most were a dark brown colour, almost like massive strips of thick liquorice.

This tree had a flat appearance with branches spreading out like the spokes of an umbrella. In most cases the trunk was formed in such a way as to make it a great climbing tree for the children. It was a flamboyant tree and there happened to be one in the front garden of the Big House.

In our new garden there was also a plethora of fruit trees bearing avocado pears, lemons, lychees, *naartjies* (pronounced 'narchie', a South African word, depicting any small, thin skinned orange, such as a satsuma, mandarin or tangerine) and a huge mulberry tree.

One of the many ways in which the Big House varied from the Little House was that it actually had a 'view'. The front garden sloped slightly downhill, so you could see over the high garden wall from inside the house, though the vista wasn't fantastic.

Opposite our road was some open ground the size of about four or five football fields, though any resemblance to such ended there. I was told this slightly marshy place, of which there were many dotted around, is known as a *vlei* (pronounced flay). The locals used it as a sort of allotment, to grow mostly mealies (sweetcorn) and occasionally watermelons and other stuff. Some way off, on the other side of the *vlei*, were more walled-in houses.

The location of the new cobalt processing plant where Ziggy was working was on the other side of the city to our home and bordered the Nkana West housing area, which lay south-west of the city centre. In fact his office consisted of one of the houses left standing after the site was cleared to make way for the new plant. Beyond that lay the mine, with all its accompanying 'topside', slag heaps, tailings dams and other such mining related stuff.

The slag heaps were large, flat-topped black hills with steep, ribbed sides where the slag slid down. The tipping of the slag from the trains, which were railed along the very edge of the dump, was a wondrous sight to behold, especially at night. The red-hot slag slowly slithered down the slopes of the man-made mountain like luminous orange icing dripping thickly down the sides of an enormous chocolate cake.

Further away from the city centre and the suburbs accommodating the ex-pats and better-off Zambians, were the townships and compounds. I knew nothing about these, other than they were where the poorer Zambians (servants, mine labourers, etc) appeared to live. I was advised these were not places where a *mzungu* madam would go, so I remained unenlightened on the subject.

October 1980
Dear Cathy, my best friend of all time,
Thanks for your letters, even though I had trouble figuring them out. I've just read them again and worked out where I went wrong. The one you wrote on the 9th arrived here two days before the one you posted on the 6th. No wonder I couldn't understand what you were rabbiting on about.

In my previous letters to everybody I'd mentioned the hazards of the spiders on the ceiling, lizards in the lounge and bull-frogs in the back-yard, but the other day I really freaked out when, as I sat minding my own business, I noticed we had cockroaches in the kitchen.

It was only when I saw those cockroaches that I realised I had never seen one before. What I used to think were cockroaches had, in fact, been earwigs.

And BIG? Oh my, they were disgusting. They were about three inches long and a good inch across. I had hopped and skipped around the kitchen with a can of Killerspray, trying to paralyse them, and once the fumes took effect they flipped over on their backs and clattered across the floor flapping their wings (I didn't know cockroaches had wings).

The noise these things made as they rattled over the tiles could only be compared to a lively performance by a large troupe of tap-dancers.

One afternoon Sandy came into the lounge with a huge, green, live grasshopper sitting on his white jacket. URGH. Assuring Brad that it was harmless, he picked it off his lapel and offered it to the poor kid, who naturally ran away. It wasn't until Brad turned to look back at Sandy that I noticed the old man had stuck the damn thing onto the back of Brad's t-shirt. Feeling slightly sick on the child's behalf, I asked Sandy to take it off. Until I opened my big mouth, Brad had not realised it was there. He panicked and raced towards me.

I yelled at him to go back to Sandy, at whom we were both screaming to remove the bloody thing, which he did and promptly put it on the dining table and walked out.

Brad and I then had a prolonged argument over why I wouldn't go and get him a drink of orange pop – I would need to go past the grasshopper which by then had jumped off the table onto the floor near the kitchen door.

What seemed like an age later Sandy came back in and removed it, muttering something about eating it. Urgh!

On another night after everyone had gone to bed, I stayed up to finish writing letters, and as I was hammering away at my Remington I heard an awful racket coming from the front door. I had heard tapping noises earlier and assumed it was the dog knocking against the door as she was scratching herself, but when I eventually went to check, she was nowhere near it.

A while later the noise sounded like it was coming from *inside*. There was a narrow, curtained window beside the door and I thought I saw a movement.

Suddenly something shot up the wall by the door with such a fluttering and clicking noise, that I nearly had a heart attack. It then leapt about eight feet in the air and landed in the middle of the lounge. Eventually I plucked up the courage to go and see what it was.

I crept to within four feet of it, which was good enough for me. It looked like a huge locust, almost four inches long, not counting the feelers, and dark brown in colour, which made it a bit difficult to see clearly, as the carpet was brown.

What I couldn't quite figure out was how the devil it got inside in the first place, unless it had crawled under the door, which seemed highly unlikely given its size.

Contrary to previous practise, I had now abandoned the habit of killing most creepy crawlies. This was for the simple reason that, apart from wasps and flies, the majority were so big that if you squashed one it made a hideous crunching sound like someone stomping on a packet of crisps. Besides that, there were too damn many of them.

This particular beastie crawled back to the door and I went over to see if I dare unlock the door to let it out as I didn't much care for the idea of leaving it overnight, not knowing where it might be in the morning. But recalling the extent of its earlier leap I elected against that idea in case it chose to flex its muscles whilst I was standing nearby. What's more, the rest of its family could have been waiting outside to come in! I gave up on my writing and went to bed. It was nowhere to be seen the following morning.

Cathy had asked in one of her letters if I had learned the local lingo yet. I had to confess that I had not because I am lousy at languages. This fact became apparent when after going on holiday for several consecutive years to Mallorca I had only managed to absorb about a dozen words of Spanish. Shameful – I know.

Fortunately the official language of Zambia is actually English, though they also have several African languages from the different regions of the country. The ones most used in our area were Bemba and Nyanja.

I went to great lengths to describe to her the pronunciation of some Zambian words.

Okay, Cathy, here we go.
For a start, lots of words ending in the letter 'e'

45

get pronounced 'ay'. You would expect Kitwe to be pronounced Kitwee, whereas the locals say Kitway.

Then there are words starting with double consonants. There are lots of those. Words like kwacha — our currency, is quite straight forward. But ngwe (coinage) is not so simple. It is not pronounced engwe or ingwe, or nugwe. The letter 'n' is just that. N-gwe. Like the nearest city to Kitwe is Ndola. N-dola, not Endola or Nadola. Wow, this is difficult to put down on paper. Let's forget about pronunciation shall we? I'll just give you a few words.

The word Muntu means a person, generally black. Our houseboy might come to me and say, "Madam, there's a muntu at the gate selling vegetables." Now if Brad were to come to me and say, "Mummy, there's a munt at the gate selling spuds," that would be totally unacceptable. The word munt on its own is considered derogatory.

Another word soon picked up was Mzungu, which means a white person.

Then there's Iwe (pronounced ee-way). Strictly speaking it means 'you'. If you wanted to attract the attention of an unknown local person walking nearby you would call 'iwe' and he'd turn around to find out what you wanted. It's like calling out 'hey you" though in a non-offensive way.

I hope you are now clear on all that. I shall be asking questions later.

X Ann

I soon found that the one word you did not call a Zambian person is 'stupid'. You could tell a man that his mother is an ugly, one eared, three-legged jackal and he probably wouldn't bat an eyelid, but to call him 'stupid' was the ultimate insult and could even land you in gaol. Given that some people we encountered could be a bit slow on the uptake, one had to be extremely careful not to use the 's' word.

One of the things which made me feel uncomfortable to start with was the custom of constantly being called 'Madam'. There is nothing odd about it in a public place like a shop or hotel, but in my own home it was totally alien. But it was the norm for house servants to call the lady of the house Madam and the man *bwana*. Some of the older servants would refer to the man of the house as Master, a term we were not at all happy with, as it seemed very 'slavish'.

It seemed there were a lot of things which would take some getting used to. However, one aspect which we had no trouble attuning to was the diversity of the social life.

One weekend we were introduced to Mindola Dam where the Rokana Sailing and Boating Club was based, and where the Copperbelt version of It's-a -Knockout was being staged.

The dam was about twelve kilometres from our house on the west side of Kitwe and someone organised for a gang of us to meet up there. Huge, circular thatched shelters, or *rondavels*, were scattered about the place as well as several *braai* boxes for use by visitors.

'Braai', pronounced 'bry' as in 'dry' is the South African word for barbecue, and a *braai* box usually consisted of a large oil drum sliced in half lengthwise, with holes punched in it and four legs welded to it. Then a sheet of strong expanded metal mesh would be placed on top to lay the meat on.

Armed with our steaks and salads we arrived there to find that virtually the entire expatriate population of Kitwe was supporting the event and nearly all the *braai* boxes had already been nabbed. Fortunately we managed to lay claim to one of the *rondavels*.

There were ten of us altogether, excluding kids. Three of the couples had brought along some cane garden furniture and a *braai* box as back-up. Unfortunately the *rondavel* wasn't big enough to accommodate the furniture and all the people, so we had to take turns sitting out in the sun.

The It's-a-Knockout competition was very well organised. The teams were made up of employees of the various companies operating in and around Kitwe. We wandered around to watch the various, often hilarious, events which included the usual jousting on a pole, racing on stilts through a maze of beer crates, walk the plank blindfolded, and many more. The kids were a bit puzzled by all this. They couldn't understand why grown-ups were playing the sort of games normally associated with children, but on a bigger scale. They took some convincing that they couldn't join in (and I wouldn't have minded a shot at a few of them myself). We eventually strolled back to the *rondavel* and got around to cooking our food at about 4:00pm.

Ziggy and I were given the privilege of using the *braai* first in view of the fact that we had the youngest children. That turned out to be more fortuitous than we had anticipated, because just as we sat down to eat, the heavens opened.

Chaos ensued as everyone tried to squeeze everything, including themselves, inside the area protected by the thatched roof.

Within three minutes we had twelve adults (I'm not sure where the extra two came from), eight chairs, five kids, a pushchair, two tables, six coolbags, two coolboxes, a beer crate and a potty - all crammed under the twelve-foot diameter roof.

This was all except the poor sod who was stuck out in the rain trying to cook food. He figured if he wedged everyone's meat onto the grill it would stop the rain putting the fire out. It continued to rain as the multitudes struggled to eat in the cramped space. As the last mouthful was devoured, the rain stopped. Bloody typical.

We stayed there until about six o'clock, but left before everyone else as we'd had enough excitement for one day.

9

October 1980
Dear All,

You know a couple of letters ago we were talking about rain?

Well, we used to think we got a fair bit of rain in England. Believe me, it bears no resemblance to the rain they get here. I was sitting in the lounge late yesterday afternoon when I heard a large pitter-patter coming from above. It sounded like half a dozen cats were dancing the cha-cha-cha on the corrugated roof. Then it got louder and louder and LOUDER until any conversation (should you be having one) became impossible to hear.

I can only liken it to lying under an overturned tin bath with someone firing marbles onto it with a pebble-dash machine. Not that I have actually experienced such an event, but as I believe I've mentioned before, I do have a pretty wild imagination. The din became so frightful that I thought the roof was going to collapse. Fifteen minutes later it went suddenly quiet — I thought I'd gone deaf. The rain had stopped and the sun came out.

After that experience I was gratified with the knowledge that the Big House has a normal, safe and sound (proofed), tiled roof.

As luck would have it we haven't had too many rainy days yet but knowing that these are soon to be expected in greater quantities we are making the most of the sunny ones.

One of these sunny days was particularly memorable, but for all the wrong reasons.

As usual, it was a lovely day and the kids and I congregated once again at the poolside of the Little Theatre. The sky was a stunning, sharp blue disturbed only by the odd white fluffy cloud wafting gently across the skyscape. The recent rainfall had perked up the green of the trees surrounding the pool area and some bright crimson flowers were showing off their newly developed petals.

Six or seven families were scattered around the pool, utilising the white tables and chairs or were spread out on towels on the narrow lawns. Being a weekday, the theatre's bar was relatively quiet as most of the men were at work, so an obliging barman took on the duties of waiter, serving drinks to the sun-lovers outside.

The kids had spent a good twenty minutes splashing about in the pool and now pursued other interests. We could hear the laughter of all the youngsters as they happily entertained themselves in the playground.

I stretched out on a beach towel, my head propped up on a pillow of discarded, folded clothes and settled down to read a novel I had borrowed from a friend. It was a perfect afternoon.

Suddenly there was a frantic cry. A voice screamed, "There's a baby in the pool!"

I leapt up from my prone position some three metres from the pool and looked across. Vicki was floating face-down, arms outstretched and totally motionless on top of the still water in the centre of the deep end.

With a single bound I was airborne. I dived into the water, reaching Vicki as I broke the surface of the pool. Arm outstretched I held her limp body out of the water whilst with the other arm I struggled to swim to the nearest pool's edge. On the side, other mothers waited to take her from me. I was out and by her side before they had finished laying her on a towel. I tried to remember the first aid training I was taught at school.

Laid on her back, I started to push down on her rib-cage, then to pump her arms up and down. It was all I could remember from fifteen years ago. I pushed and pumped, pushed and pumped, expecting to see water flow out of her mouth. Nothing happened.

I screamed at those around me.

"Please, I don't know what I'm doing. This isn't working. For God's sake, find someone who knows what to do!"

One of the mums had already rushed into the bar to alert the few members in there to the situation and was closely followed out by Glyn, the guy who had signed us into the theatre that very first night on our wedding anniversary. He took over from me, performing the same ritual, also to no avail. Hands held me back.

After what seemed like hours, but must have been no more than a minute, a stranger came staggering along.

Shouting unintelligibly he pushed everyone out of the way, hauled a distraught Glyn off Vicki and got down on his knees. He then started performing the mouth to mouth procedure.

I wasn't aware how long this went on, but there was total silence as the drunken helper rhythmically forced air into Vicki. Suddenly he spat crudely onto the concrete floor and a few seconds later there was a cacophony of cheering voices as Vicki began to cough, puking out mouthfuls of chlorinated water.

As Vicki, wrapped in a warm towel, was passed across to me, I held her tight and rocked her precious body with the most amazing relief whilst I wept with gratitude at having my beautiful daughter returned to me.

As emotions eventually calmed down someone wisely suggested that

Vicki should be taken to the Company Clinic (the Medical Centre which we were assigned to) for a check-up. Ziggy was phoned at work and came tearing across town to take us there as quickly as possible.

At the Clinic, the staff lauded the swift actions of our knowledgeable first-aider, saying that Vicki's internal temperature intimated that she had absorbed a considerable quantity of pool water and had been saved 'just in time'.

They ordered me to hold Vicki close (yeah, like I was likely to let her go?) and spoon fed her sweet tea as hot as she could take it, to warm her up inside and impede the possible onset of pneumonia.

After about an hour and another temperature check, they were happy for us to go home.

Whilst I had been tending to Vicki, Ziggy briefly returned to the Theatre Club to collect Brad and Leon who had remained under the care of assorted mums, and to speak to, and thank, Vicki's mortal guardian angel.

The stranger, an Australian named Patrick, had arrived at the theatre an hour before Vicki's incident and was slowly getting smashed. It transpired that he had driven up from Lusaka that morning and as he neared Luansha, some 50km south-east of Kitwe, he came across a dreadful, very recent, traffic accident. A Range Rover taking a bend had rolled several times, landing on its roof. The wheels were still spinning when he arrived.

Together with other passing motorists he helped to get the couple out of the overturned vehicle. But tragedy had struck. On the back seat of the vehicle had been a baby in a carrycot. The poor infant had been thrown from her bed and crushed by the vehicle.

Patrick had come to the theatre to drown his sorrows.

Whilst he was still dosing himself with spirits, Ziggy reckoned Patrick now seemed remarkably sober.

Over another whisky he told Ziggy, "The sweetest thing I have ever tasted in my entire life, was when your little girl puked into my mouth."

Ziggy returned to the Clinic to fetch Vicki and me, then took us all home. The doctor had told us to keep a close watch on Vicki that night for any signs of distress or of sleep turning to coma and if she showed any signs of irregular or shallow breathing, we were to contact them immediately. Needless to say, neither Ziggy nor I got much sleep that night.

Vicki woke up next to her twin brother the following morning, bright and cheerful as if nothing had happened. After getting everyone dressed we went through for breakfast.

On his way out the door, Ziggy turned to Vicki and asked, "What would you like to do today, my precious?"

Without a moment's pause, she replied, "I'd like to go swimming please."

10

October 1980
Dear All,
After doing some bitching about a sudden change in the
weather I was soon eating my words. One morning dawned
bright and sunny so after the usual shopping expedition,
the kids and I retired to the Theatre Club's swimming
pool. Between cooling swims I stretched out on a towel
and it was so hot it felt as if I were standing in front
of a roaring log fire.
After a while I felt the backs of my legs tingling and
thought "funny". A trip to the Ladies and a contorted
glance in a mirror revealed the cause of my discomfort. I
had a broad, bright red streak down the back of each leg.
Like the twit that I am, I never dreamt that, having
spent so much time in the sun at every opportunity as a
teenager, its rays could still affect me so dramatically.
Obviously I hadn't reckoned on the heat of the midday sun
thirteen degrees south of the equator. For the remainder
of the day I slopped around like a walking oil slick,
having applied half a bottle of Johnson's Baby Oil to my
dried-out skin.
I knew I would have felt a real idiot if we'd had
badminton that night with my whiter than white, newly
made, tennis skirt and my redder than red, freshly fried
legs. As it happens, external evening activities have all
been put on hold.

I received a phone call from my badminton buddy advising that we would not
be playing that week as the Zambian government had gone into crisis mode
and a curfew was being imposed. My friend told me that it was because of
the forthcoming 'long weekend', a public holiday celebrating Zambia
Independence Day. The powers-that-be, she said, had decided that the local
populous got so excited (read that as drunk and disorderly) that the
Government proposed a curfew from dusk till dawn in order to maintain
control of any miscreants.

That was all very well, but what about us good upstanding citizens who
just wanted to go out for a friendly game of shuttlecocking, I wanted to
know?

Ziggy, on the other hand, reckoned it was all just a ploy to take people's attention away from the massive shortages they were forced to endure.

However there was an upside. The good thing to emerge from curfew was that you got hubby home earlier than usual from his post-work pint at the Club. Remarkably, Ziggy arrived home just after six o'clock on that first day because they had stopped serving drinks at 5:30 and thrown everyone out of the bar twenty minutes later to give the staff plenty of time to get home before the start of the curfew.

And he was definitely in favour, as he had the good sense to call at the liquor store and pick up a bottle of whisky to sustain us through the night. What a bright lad.

Luckily the restrictions did not stop us from going out at the weekend. Starting perhaps a little sooner than normal, we took all our gear down to the Club where a large gang of folk had gathered for a *braai*.

Whilst we stood around chatting, eating and generally getting pissed, the kids (now constantly protected by armbands) enjoyed themselves splashing about in the pool. Brad had us in fits of laughter at his attempts to jump in the deep end – backwards. It wasn't so much the jumping in backwards that caused the merriment, as much as the fact that he tried to *run* backwards before doing it. How he never cracked his chin on the edge of the pool during this bizarre routine I would never know.

By now Leon had graduated to jumping into the pool as long as I was in the immediate vicinity to assist him if need be. Vicki would still only jump in if I was in the water and held both her hands. Then she would scream blue murder if I let go of her before she had done a one-handed doggy-paddle to the steps.

As for the curfew, both explanations I had been given were a load of old cobblers. The truth was that there had been an attempted coup and that was why the government imposed a curfew. And it lasted for four weeks.

During that time we had quite a scary experience early one evening.

We were driving back from somewhere out of town, down a fairly empty stretch of road, when we came across a roadblock.

The word 'roadblock' was a bit of a misnomer as the road was hardly 'blocked'. It comprised two dilapidated wooden guard huts, which actually bore a closer resemblance to outdoor toilet sheds, on either side of the road, placed about 100 metres apart. Wandering around somewhere in the general vicinity of these guardhouses would be a pair of scruffy looking Zambians (almost) dressed in camouflage gear. And they had rifles slung over their shoulders.

The rifles looked a bit like some cast-off relics from World War I, but they could probably give you a nasty sting provided they didn't explode in the soldier's face first. In any event, it was customary to stop at these posts when flagged down by the soldier waving his weapon around as though attempting to swat a fly.

Ziggy stopped the car about fifty metres short of the road block .

"Let's make the bugger walk," he said, as one of the government's military representatives sauntered along the road to greet us.

Having casually un-straightened his beret en route, he leant against the driver's door and peered in through the open window, complete with the rifle barrel. He slowly scanned the interior of the car for any signs of hidden weapons or tanks, then turned his attention to Ziggy.

Cocking his nose towards the sky and casting glances around him, the soldier said, in a very gruff voice, "You got any secrets?"

"What?" said Ziggy.

"You got any secrets?"

"No," Ziggy replied.

The soldier leaned further inside the car. He looked at the dashboard.

"You *sure* you got no secrets?"

Ziggy looked at him (not too arrogantly) and repeated, "No, I do not have any secrets."

Then he looked past Ziggy towards me.

"You! You got any secrets?"

I was crapping myself, and like Ziggy I responded, "No."

He extricated himself from Ziggy's window and took a step back. Never taking his eyes from the car, he walked casually around the front until he reached my door, where he tapped on the glass with the muzzle of his rifle. Trying not to make any sudden movements I slowly wound the window down.

With a heavy sigh he shoved his head inside the car until he was so close to me I could count the hairs in his ears. Leaning in even closer he scanned the area under the dashboard and by the handbrake between the seats before slowly reversing his body out.

With another swaggering stroll he returned to Ziggy's window where he leaned heavily against the wing mirror and expelled a long breath before transferring his rifle from one hand to the other.

Now getting quite concerned, Ziggy asked him, in a slightly quavering voice, "What sort of secrets are you talking about?"

Raising his eyebrows whilst gesticulating with his fingers towards his mouth, he said, "Anything. Marlboro, Rothmans, Camel. ANY secrets."

With an inaudible sigh of relief, Ziggy assured him that we didn't have any secrets at all, as neither of us smoked cigarettes.

At this the soldier stood back, looked down at us in disgust and – using the barrel of his sturdy rifle – pointed us forward toward the direction in which we wanted to go.

The onset of the curfew clashed spectacularly with the opening of the Olde Time Music Hall which was fully sold out for the first three nights. A lot of work had gone into the production and some turns were hilariously funny. Although those participating were all amateurs, they were remarkably good.

We had hoped that the curfew palaver would be curtailed after the Independence celebrations and 'normal service could be resumed' but alas, no.

The best the Little Theatre could do was to put on matinee performances on the three weekends, which was not very convenient for participating members or for any audience with small children, as this wasn't exactly a family show.

Once the stupid curfew was lifted, our social life returned to some semblance of normality.

If anything about our lives could be called normal.

11

The Little House
Oct 1980
Dear All,

> Ten more hours to go,
> Ten more hours to go,
>   eee-aye-addio
> Ten more hours to go.

Yes, you have guessed it, we move into the Big House tomorrow.

I've just been sitting outside for half an hour and it was lovely relaxing in the warm breeze, quite dark apart from a skyful of stars and the glow of a neighbour's security lights.

The only sounds came from an assortment of insects and night-birds and the occasional bark of a distant dog. I could have sat there enjoying that for hours, but thought it would be a good idea to write a few words to our temporary-home benefactors. I shall include a copy to you as the letter mentions some things I don't recall telling you about, and can't be bothered to check my copy letters.

Did I ever tell you that I have been keeping carbon copies of all my letters? No? I didn't think I had. The fact is, it got that I couldn't remember what I had said to whom in the various letters I sent out, and didn't want to waste time repeating myself, so decided to keep carbon copies of my missives, which I could refer to before starting a new letter. Ziggy reckons this habit is probably attributed to my experience as a legal secretary for so many years, where you had to keep copies of everything.

Before I push off to bed, I must quickly tell you about last night.

At approximately fifteen minutes to seven we were quietly watching an American sit com on the telly when the screen went blank in mid-sentence. After a while an unseen voice announced that the next programme would be following shortly.

After a couple of minutes a notice appeared on the screen with the words 'Before the news, here is an interlude of music'. This was followed by ten minutes of TOTAL SILENCE. Ah, the wonders of ZTV.

It is commonly acknowledged that Zambian television is the eighth wonder of the world. I can verify that — it is a wonder it ever gets on the air.

For all that, I shall miss this television when we move into our own place because, as you know, a TV is one of the few things we did not pack in the crates.

Anyway, where was I? Oh yes, that letter to Sharon and Rob. Here it is…

Dear Sharon and Rob,

Many thanks for the use of your home whilst you've been away.

Knowing my children and their knack of breaking things I brought along plastic plates, dishes and cups for their use. Unfortunately we still managed to break one of your cups and one small plate, sincere apologies. If you will arrange replacements of your choice we will gladly pay for them.

We had heard a lot of barking and whistle-blowing one night and wondered who was having problems with security. Apparently it was us. Fortunately Nina saw them off before they could get over the fence.

The guard across the road later explained that he had seen the would-be burglars climbing the trees in order to get over our front fence, so started blowing his whistle. He said it was not the first time an attempt had been made to gain entry in this way. The next day we got Ronald to lop off all branches which overhung the fence into the garden. We hope we did the right thing.

Another precaution we felt necessary, was the removal of your new lounge suite. We didn't like the thought of being responsible for any damage to it, caused by our three little angels, so we moved it out to the safety of the kaya and brought in our own.

We also brought in quite a lot of other bits and pieces - toys, towels, household items, etc. As far as possible we have collected up and removed them. If, however, you come across any strange objects, perhaps you would be good enough to give me a call and we will then collect.

The most unhappy event to report concerns Utsi. We are

very sorry and sad to have to tell you that she was
involved in a road accident and killed sometime in the
early hours of Sunday the 5th October.

Each night she was 'asked' if she wanted to come
inside. Some nights she didn't appear at the door at all.
This was one of those nights, and the next morning Ziggy
found her lying at the side of the road. The only
consolation is that she appeared to have been killed
outright, so hopefully didn't suffer.

We were all terribly upset, as we had grown very fond
of Utsi in that short time. Unfortunately, there was
nothing we could have done to avoid such an incident,
other than lock her in the house 24 hours a day.

I cannot think of anything else, except to say that if
you can't find anything then give us a call - the chances
are we've hidden it.

Once again, very many thanks for the use of your home.
Sincerely, Ziggy, Ann & children.

In case you are curious about the extent of these Aladdin's Cave crates I mentioned earlier, I shall expand.

Way back in 1971 at the grand old age of 21, I went to live in Toronto, Canada with my best mate Pip. Even in those days I was keen on sewing and acknowledging that my sewing machine would hardly fit inside my suitcase, I sea-freighted it across the Atlantic in a trunk, in which I also chucked a few personal items. Those things did help make me feel more at home at the time even if our emigration was short-lived. I returned to England after ten months where I resumed my relationship with Ziggy and we eventually got married.

As a result of my Canadian experience, I knew how important it was to take as many of our belongings as possible to Zambia. This was, after all, a two year contract, with the possibility of an extension for a further two years. The only things we left in storage in England were our collection of lead crystal ornaments and glasses (wedding gifts), our do-it-yourself equipment, and our furniture and curtains.

It may seem impossible to believe, but even without the big stuff we packed *thirteen* full crates of possessions. The company were paying for five to be shipped, which anyone would think should be more than adequate. But we managed to fill an additional eight, the cost of which we covered ourselves. And we are not talking about small crates here.

There were five 'long' wooden crates equivalent to the size of a coffin needed for a short fat person (though not coffin-shaped, of course). The remainder were about 2ft square by 3ft high.

The contents of this considerable collection consisted of:
• All bedding, including pillows and duvets, sufficient for a double and three single beds

- Surround stereo hi-fi unit of which the front speakers were rather large, together with all our records and tapes
- Swimming and bath towels
- Bathroom items, toiletries and extensive first aid kit
- Loads of reference books (cookery, dictionary, atlas, etc.)
- Children's books.

The kids' toys alone would have filled one large crate, except we split them between several crates, as we did with clothes which couldn't be accommodated in our suitcases.

In fact many things of a similar ilk were spread through various crates just in case one got damaged in transit or fell into the sea. We were obeying the 'don't put all your eggs in one basket' rule.

By far the most comprehensive contents came from our kitchen cupboards. Pyrex casserole dishes and mixing bowls, jugs, our full collection of stainless steel saucepans and lids, colanders, rolling pin, sieves and all my baking trays, patty and cake tins, cooling racks and roasting tins, and non-stick frying pans. Even my large, old-fashioned pressure cooker, which proved to be invaluable.

Then of course there was our full six-setting dinner service with serving dishes and matching tea set, as well as a separate Cornishware 28-piece breakfast set. Our dining cutlery and large assortment of kitchen utensils was also quite extensive. And whilst we could probably have acquired them locally, we figured we might as well take our array of casual drinking glasses along too.

I also packed two clocks, a hall mirror, some small pictures, a few treasured ornaments, and several framed photographs. Last, but not least was our rather nice Christmas tree and decorations.

I imagine that any clarification needed regarding the degree of my insanity has now gone totally out of the window.

29th October 1980
'The Big House'
Plot 3062, McFrazier Road, Kitwe.
Dear All,
Ohh, the feather and down pillows. Ohh, the comfort of the mattress. Ahh, the bliss of the soft duvet. And yuk, having to make breakfast!

It was utter mayhem yesterday morning, being the first work-day breakfast I'd had to prepare for eight weeks. It was also the most un-birthday-like birthday I have ever had.

To start with I had tossed and turned all Monday night. It must have been the shock of the comfortable bed. The kids got up at the same time as Ziggy — 6am - and by the time we had taken showers or had washes, got dressed, etc, I only had time for a quick cup of tea before taking Ziggy to work, so I could have the car.

It wasn't until he passed me three cards, which had been posted to his office, and wished me "Happy Birthday", that I remembered it was 'that' day. I returned to the breakfast scene and birthdays were immediately forgotten in the rush to get everything organised before collecting my friend, Lou, for a shopping trip. That was a complete waste of time as we couldn't find any decent beef, or soap and I forgot to buy the shower curtain, paw-paw and booze.

But I'm jumping ahead of myself. To quote from the Sound of Music, let's start at the very beginning.

That last Monday of October 1980 was rather hectic as we vacated our temporary home. Suitcases had to be repacked with everyone's clothes. For the life of me I could not figure out how I had managed to fit them all into the luggage when we travelled to Africa, what seemed like months ago. But that challenge was nothing compared to locating and packing the household and personal belongings we had brought from the Big House, which had intermingled with Sharon and Rob's possessions. Tracking down all of the kids' toys was a nightmare.

We dumped everything at the Big House and after lunch the day took on a different slant. I spent the afternoon scooting between Jambo Drive (the

Little House), the Big House and the dog kennels.

A couple of weeks after we had arrived in Kitwe, Molly had expounded the virtues of having a dog or dogs on the premises. She told me about a friend of hers who was leaving Zambia and who was looking for a home for her old Irish Setter bitch. Molly operated on the theory of 'the more the merrier' and also managed to persuade me to purchase, at great expense, a pedigree Irish Setter puppy born the week before. This litter of eight pups just happened to have been sired by her own Setter.

The idea, she said, is that the older dog teaches the young dog the ropes. There is also the advantage of keeping one dog outdoors and the other indoors. If the 'outdoor' dog gets knobbled by intruders you still have the 'indoor dog' to raise the alarm. Not a very comforting concept. Still it did have a logical air to it, and since she was the owner of five assorted canines and had not had a robbery in years, the plan was approved.

As we were still in the leave house when all this was agreed, we had to arrange for the old dog to go into kennels for four or five weeks until we moved into our own place. The puppy had needed to stay with its mother for several more weeks anyway.

Now all these dogs needed collecting. It felt like there where more than two of them as the people concerned with the hand-over were out, but after three abortive attempts I eventually managed to collect the big dog, Brandy. She assertively sprawled on the back seat of the car hardly leaving enough room for the children. On the way to collect the puppy, Brandy decided she'd prefer to stand up and proceeded to slobber profusely down my neck. Next we collected a bundle of tan-coloured canine fluff, which was mortified by the sight of the great hairy monster and three kids and promptly wedged itself between the passenger seat and door where it remained throughout the entire journey home.

Once we hit base, Brandy tore about the garden like a two-year-old at the sheer delight of being back in a residential environment. Having been restricted to the confines of a pen since his birth, the puppy was right behind her. Deciding on a name for the pup was the next problem.

He had a fancy pedigree name but one was hardly inclined to refer to him as Roscarbury's Ruby Prince on a daily basis. A 'pet' name needed to be decided upon. We refused to call him the obvious 'Prince' and decided it had to be something that went with Brandy.

The previous week we had gone through various possibilities. Soda was the natural choice, but we felt it sounded a bit bland and soppy for a boy dog. Ziggy suggested Ice, but I developed a weird vision of the poor mite melting into a reddy-brown puddle in the midday sun.

I was on my way to bed on Monday night when Ziggy said, "What about Coke?"

"There are four bottles in the fridge."

"No, no, no. Coke for the dog."

I thought, *he's finally cracked.*

"NO," he persisted, "call the dog 'Coke'."

And so it was.

The kids latched onto this new name very quickly and Brandy and Coke played very happily together. We had a big problem keeping Brandy out of the house, which we deemed a necessity due to her hairy paws resembling floor mops, which left plate-sized muddy splodges every time she came in if it was wet outside.

However, the whole idea of the combination of old and young dogs began to weaken as we never heard a peep out of Brandy. Even when every other dog in the neighbourhood barked at the sound of locals wandering past after dark, Brandy remained silent. We were beginning to wonder if at some stage in her life she'd had her vocal chords removed.

My Tuesday birthday was a disaster. After the useless shopping trip, I collected a new friend, Margaret, who happened to live ten houses from us, then we all went back to Lou's flat for coffee. By the time we arrived I was far too hot to drink coffee, so Lou offered me a cold drink instead. The most exciting thing she had was orange squash. Now, I ask you, is that any way to treat a lady on her birthday? I declined a second.

Once home I had only twenty five minutes in which to prepare lunch before Ziggy arrived. The meat wasn't completely thawed and Foster was using the main kitchen worktop as an ironing board, standing right in front of the cupboards that contained things I needed to get to. The stupid bugger wouldn't dream of packing up until after lunch but was happy to see me fumbling around him until, in the end, I had to tell him to shift all his things before I beat him about the head with the frying pan.

Lunch went reasonably well under the circumstances, although the steak was a trifle more rare that we usually take it. Vicki was being a pain, deciding she did not want to eat her tomato, or her lettuce nor, later, her meat. She was sent to bed twice during the course of lunch, promising to eat it all up if I let her come back. But she didn't.

Ziggy had borrowed one of the company vanettes (the local name for a small, open-backed van) in order to get home for lunch but when he came to leave he couldn't get the damn thing started. So he had to take the car which meant I couldn't finish my shopping. However, he did agree to pick up some booze on the way home.

I spent the rest of the afternoon sorting out boxes and bags, organising wardrobes and generally tidying up odds and sods. Brad couldn't understand why I hadn't made a birthday cake, but considering that we'd only finished eating *his* three days earlier I decided against it.

It was 8.30 by the time we got the kids off to bed and then came the crunch. Ziggy had forgotten to pick up the booze, so all I had to celebrate my 31st birthday in my new home was beer. Actually it wasn't even beer, it was lager and it came with two choices – drink it or don't drink it.

It was produced by National Breweries and didn't appear to have a name because there were never any labels on the bottles, though a name would have been rather superfluous given its exclusivity.

I did later discover that whilst there was only one beer, there were two versions because one brewery was in Ndola, the other in Lusaka. Fortunately we usually copped for the Ndola variety except when the brewery was experiencing mechanical problems, which it frequently did. Then the Lusaka brew would be trucked up to the Copperbelt, and it was revolting.

Personally, I thought it bore a close resemblance to liquid horse manure. The smell reminded me of the smell which emanated from a galvanised bucket of luminous, greenish-brown slop which sat in our yard when I was a kid. It was a concoction my grandmother Doris brewed to water her tomato plants in our conservatory and consisted of water to which horse manure from my pony was added.

Needless to say when the Lusaka 'beer' was in town I changed my drinking habits, even if it meant resorting to orange squash.

Years later someone else must have noticed the disparity in the brews and changed something in the brewing process, as Lusaka did eventually produce a more palatable version.

So my birthday was at least memorable, if only on a negative basis.

November 1980
Dear N,M & D,

Thank you for the birthday cards - received today. The message inside earned you a score of at least 12 points out of 10 for the 'Feet in the Mouth' spot. I quote:

"Hope you have a nice day and that Ziggy takes you out for a slap-up meal, with all the trimmings, you know, candles, wine - the lot." Unquote

As I'm sure you will by now have learnt, you could not have got much further from the truth.

Ziggy couldn't take me out anywhere due to the curfew. Had he done so there would have been absolutely no chance of candles, as they are like gold here. I have been trying to buy some ever since I found out that power cuts are very frequent in the rainy season. And as far as the wine goes … if you're prepared to pay through the nose for a bottle for something that resembles extra sweet brake fluid, then wine it is. If not, forget it.

In answer to your question Nancy, regarding the timing of your visit, I would think it better that you come out in March, before the pub staff ask for time off over Easter. I have no idea what the weather will be like then but can guarantee it will be warmer than you would be getting in the UK.

Have you noticed how, since being here, I keep referring to the place where you live as 'the UK'? When I was living in England I would not have dreamt of calling it 'the UK' but here one automatically seems to latch onto it.

Sorry, I digress.

Whenever you decide to come, make sure you give us plenty of notice so that Ziggy can arrange to have some time off whilst you are here. We thought it might be nice for us to visit a game park during your stay. Of course, that all depends on the weather. For all I know the game parks might be under four feet of water at that time.

This letter writing business is all very well, but I have so many other things to do.

Not the least of which was sewing.

Not long after we had moved in, it occurred to me that something might be amiss when I noticed I could see the solitary street light through the closed lounge curtains. So one night, when the curtains were drawn and the lights on, I nipped out to the garden to establish exactly what could be seen by anyone who may be *outside* the house. Oops.

The very nice curtains, on which I spent hours slaving over a hot sewing machine, concealed nothing. Not only could I distinctly see Ziggy walking around the lounge in his underpants, but I could also clearly make out what pattern was on them.

We had found, to our dismay, that both his dressing-gown and his bath-robe had been packed into storage in the UK, so the poor deprived (or should it be depraved) sod would have to continue walking around in his underpants for a while until I can buy or make him one.

I knew that making lined curtains was quite a tedious affair but adding lining to curtains already completed was a pain in the arse, so I was certainly not amused by the knowledge that I would then have to sew up another 27 metres of the stuff - always providing someone sold curtain lining in Kitwe.

One day Brad came trotting indoors followed closely by Vicki who, being a little snitch at the time, piped up, "Mummy, Brad's got a lizard in his hand."

Naturally I didn't believe her. Foolish me. Next minute Brad put the lizard (actually a gecko) down on the floor and we watched it scuttling around the kitchen. Really it was not as bad as it sounds, until its tail fell off when Coke pounced on it. The gecko beat a hasty, stunted retreat and the severed tail continued to wriggle. URGH. Until Coke ate it. DOUBLE URGH!!

On the subject of creepy-crawlies, on another occasion the kids called me to the front door to look at a 'mosquito'. It was five inches long. It was not a mosquito.

We had recently purchased a book entitled *Insects of Zambia* and discovered this was a stick insect. Using some blue tack, I stuck a 50p coin next to it for size comparison and took some photographs. As the name implies, it looks just like a stick. On a tree you probably wouldn't even notice it. But as we didn't normally have sticks growing out of our front door we were able to spot it quite easily.

I think I mentioned earlier that 'Brandy' and 'bark' did not fit in the same sentence. Well, we eventually heard her do so but only because Coke was biting her. The little sod would run up behind her and sink his teeth into a clump of matted hair (of which she had many) or grab her tail and pull it like they were playing doggy tug'o'war. Brandy would stand just so much then try to run away. With the puppy firmly attached to her backside, she obviously didn't get very far and so resorted to barking and growling at him.

If Brandy wasn't handy, Coke would try to bite what/whomsoever was. He mostly went for the ankles or calves, but in the case of Vicki he took a liking to her fat little bottom. I was in fits of laughter one afternoon watching him chase her up and down the garden, Vicki attempting to outrun him, but standing little chance. But the funniest sight of all was Coke with Leon.

Leon had been playing in the paddling pool and as usual had no clothes on. Coke was sniffing about nearby when something very tempting caught his eye, whereupon he hopped up to Leon and tried to bite his little willy. Naturally, Leon shouted and ran off. Coke found this a great game and ran after him. So there was Leon running around the garden, holding onto his spab, with Coke at his side jumping up trying to bite it. Every time he almost succeeded Leon would yell "Hey!" at the top of his voice, at which Cokey would bark. For the next few minutes all I could hear was - "pitter-patter pitter-patter, HEY, yap, yap, pitter-patter pitter-patter, HEY, yap, yap", etc.

Eventually Leon came running inside, shouting to the puppy right behind him, "HEY, you shouldn't *do* that to me!"

Coke, not to be outdone, wasn't giving up and started on Brad instead. With Brad being older and bigger I realised Coke would have more to get hold of so I called Brad inside straight away and made him put on some pants.

Nancy Darling, Mummy Dear, Source of my Life,
I would like to ask you a really BIGGG favour.
I wondered if I might put upon your kind nature and undying motherly love, and ask you to purchase a few items and send them out in a small crate. Naturally, I shall repay whatever costs are incurred. But PLEEEASE, help me.
A lot of this might seem insignificant to you, but all things considered, they could make life a lot easier and happier. I shall make a list !!!
- The largest jar of Marmite and bottle of brown sauce you can find; Garlic Salt (several packets). Also some Worcestershire Sauce and red food colouring — and any other colour of interest;
- Some paper cake cases; a box of cling film and one of aluminium foil (largest in both cases). Freezer labels. I know, sounds stupid, but could you get 2 or 3 packs of those small oblong ones.
- Blutack. (they've not heard of it in the stationery shops here) and a 1981 Calendar - One of the ones you usually get from Boots that I can make notes on.
- A tea strainer. I forgot to put ours in my suitcase after breakfast the morning we left and it is probably easier to buy a new one than go through our stored stuff. We don't get teabags here, so I really need one cos if I get tea dregs in my mouth it makes me gag.
- I was going to ask for bay leaves, but just heard that one of our mates has a bush of them as big as an oak tree!
- Dog collar. No I don't mean crate up the vicar! A normal collar to fit a very hairy, fully grown Irish Setter for when Coke is bigger, also a choker chain and a leash. I'm trying to do some obedience training with him, but the little bugger keeps biting through the rope I'm using.
- Delia Smith #3. I don't know if it'll be out yet, but we have the DS Cookery Course books I & II, and you won't believe how much we use them. If it's not available yet, please bring it with you when you come out on holiday.

- Cassette Tapes- blanks and some easy-listening stuff; and ANYTHING by the Muppets.

- Socks - any colour for the kids. But more in need are knee length socks for Ziggy to wear on site — any colour apart from black! For saying that the majority of the engineering personnel go to work in formal shorts and long socks, it's amazing that the latter are not available here. (I can make virtually anything in clothes, but not socks. Even if I could, the crimplene would keep sliding down his legs.)

- You know that little flat fan heater you have, which you never use? If it's unlikely you'll want to use it is there any chance we could have it? It would just do to take the chill off the air on winter nights, which I am told can last for up to four weeks!

And that's about it. The correct method of sending out the box, complete with required paperwork, is essential. I have put the information you will need on a separate sheet of paper, which you can keep on one side until you have everything put together. If there is any chance you could send it in time for Christmas, that would be GREAT.

If I think of anything before you've finished packing it, I shall let you know. (Oh, please not, I hear you say.)

Please make a note of everything you spend, together with cost of freightage. I shall send you a cheque from our UK bank account to cover all costs.

Thank you darling mother.

16 McFrazier Crescent, Kitwe.
November 1980
Dear Everyone,

Before you ask - I know that the above is not the address I originally gave to you. It was only when two men came along from the local council to cut off our water supply that I found out where we really live.

Anyway, that matters not to you, as you must still always address mail to the Post Box number as it would appear that street deliveries only occur about twice a year.

zz p 11   g

a   =

Ah, I see that in my absence to go to the loo, Vicki has been practising her typing.

On the subject of kids, the little buggers have been driving me mad. They have done nothing this afternoon but scrap, fall out, cry to go out, cry to come in and have fetched out every bloody toy they possess, leaving them scattered on the passage and kitchen floors.

Peace. I've just threatened the lot of 'em that if they don't shut up and stop arguing that black is white and white is black then I'll stick my feet up each of their backsides and they'll all land in bed. Brad and Leon have already had their legs slapped and Vicki's reaction at seeing this was as good as if it had happened to her too. How long the peace will last is another matter. Foster is currently creeping around as if he's too scared to tread on a feather in case it makes a noise!

I had really been looking forward to using all my own familiar stuff in the kitchen. As is my wont, the various pots, pans, dishes, utensils, etc. had been logically sorted and stored in designated cupboards in the kitchen, of which there were plenty. I clearly and slowly explained to Foster where these different types of items were stored.

Once the crate unpacking was finished I reckoned I would be able to get my act together. By the time we moved in we had all the main furniture, but were very short on bookshelf space and somewhere to put the stereo. Initially the books were piled on the shelf above the fireplace and on the floor. The stereo was artistically positioned on an empty crate.

We were getting a wall-unit made but guessed that if the Rhinestone joinery shop worked at the normal Zambian pace, we'd be stuck with the crate for a few months. The telephone sat on an up-ended laundry basket which we fortunately didn't need for that purpose as there were fitted ones in both bathrooms. The typing situation was not much better.

I put the typewriter on a coffee table, whilst I sat on the sofa with the cushions removed so I could fit my knees under the table. It was most uncomfortable. But no more so than sitting at the dining table, which was far too high to type at without resting my chin on the space bar and getting shoulder-ache from reaching for the keys.

I couldn't figure out where all my time went considering we had a servant to do the housework, although I did seem to spend a lot of time doing all the little odds and sods that Foster never quite did properly. And there were plenty.

In the kitchen I would take things out and use them, then Foster washed and dried them and put them away in *entirely different places*.

At 6.30 one morning Ziggy and I had a ten minute game of 'hunt the tea-strainer'. We eventually tracked it down in a drawer containing towels.

After putting the pots and pans back in the right places I had to sort out which of the kids clothes I could put in their wardrobes and which need be washed again – properly. Sometimes the clothes reappeared dirtier than they were before they were washed.

Foster spent about two hours every day sweeping, then washing the floors (on his knees) and up to four hours on a Friday, when he also applied polish. I figured we would soon be down to bare earth!

I asked him why he didn't use the mop, and the only reason would appear to be that it takes longer for the floors to dry, and invariably the kids were walking in and out all the time. I assured him that I would soon make sure they stayed outside if he used the mop.

But Foster seemed fixated by floors. That's all very well (I can hear you scowling in the background) but it meant he spent less time doing other jobs.

I contemplated replacing Foster. The thing that stopped me was that he seemed to be basically very honest which I was told could be a rare commodity in house-servants. When we first took him on, it was on the basis of NO accommodation.

Within two days he'd persuaded me that he had nowhere else to live and would I just let him move into the *kaya* as his family stayed elsewhere?

Next he told me that his wife and children were about to be thrown out of their accommodation, so could they stay with him in the *kaya* until he could arrange for them to go and live with his brother in Malawi?

I conceded to his request.

Then could he keep his eldest two boys with him after his wife had gone so that they could continue with their schooling? Only after agreeing to this did I discover they hadn't even started school yet.

Ever been had?

As it was, he got higher than the average pay, plus three-quarters of his food, etc.

Before we moved into the Big House he had acquired two chickens and let them have the run of the garden. Shortly after we settled in there appeared four chicks.

I was fuming. The cheeky bugger had never even asked if he could have *any* chickens running about. At that rate we would be up to our eyeballs in chicken droppings before you could say fried eggs.

After a week, one of the chicks had gone missing, so Ziggy asked the eldest boy (Sam) if they had eaten it. Sam was not very amused and said that Coke had killed it.

We could not find out from Sam what Coke had done to kill it, except that it was very dead. I wasn't too concerned myself as this lessened the volume of chicken poo to walk in, but nonetheless I suggested to him that perhaps he'd better keep his livestock secured in future.

One day I spotted the two big chickens helping themselves to the remains of Brandy's breakfast – a privilege normally enjoyed by Coke. I was just about to call for Coke to come and see them off, when the red tornado zoomed round the corner and there was snapping and puppy-barking and a flurry of feathers as the birds shot off in opposite directions to escape him.

He kept up his pursuit for about five minutes, by which time the birds must have lost whatever weight they might have gained from eating dog leftovers.

When you consider that the primary supplement to the dogs' mealie meal diet came in the form of small plastic bags of chicken feet, beaks and innards, then his penchant for trying to catch chickens was hardly surprising.

Round about that time the two dogs were due for de-worming tablets.

Coke was no problem, bar having to dodge the needle-like teeth, as I shoved it down his throat then held his mouth closed. But Brandy was something else altogether. She had to be given two tablets. What a joke.

I tried giving them to her singly – made three attempts on each one – only to have them spat straight out. I'd had my hand halfway down her throat in the process, so can only conclude that her tongue reaches as far as her arse. Then I had a brainwave. Crush them, mix with water and pour them down her throat.

With Foster holding her by the collar, me prizing her jaws open and Brad pouring the stuff into her mouth she perhaps managed to swallow the equivalent of one quarter of a tablet. Whereas I finished up covered in slobber, hairs, water and a thin white film of worming tablets.

So much for the joys of dog ownership.

In case you're wondering, they did not cut off our water (apropos beginning of this chapter). Rhinestone in their wisdom had forgotten to mention to us that it was our responsibility to go along to the appropriate authority and pay a deposit against the supply of our water. We found this most odd since Rhinestone were going to be paying the bills.

So when the said authority received a letter from the previous tenant saying that they were no longer responsible for the water bills, two little men in brown overalls were sent along to cut it off, not knowing (or caring for that matter) if anyone else had moved into the property.

I soon made sure that they cared enough to go away for a couple of days until I'd had chance to find out what on earth was going on. Suffice it to say we were soon legally watered.

15

November 1980
Dear All,

Brad started pre-school last week!

They call it pre-school rather than playschool since the emphasis is on learning as much as on playing.

It seems they get children to a low level of reading and writing before they start proper school at the age of 5. On the day I went to try and arrange for Brad's admittance to the unsuspecting establishment, which is run by the Round Table, one of the teachers even had a small group of kids doing simple sums.

On speaking to the headmistress, Mrs Forrester, it appears she is hoping to get a playschool started next January for three-year-olds. I have since asked her if I can put Vicki and Leon on her waiting list, but they will only be eligible to join in April, after they have turned three.

Anyway, on Monday 10th November Brad marched proudly along with his school bag. They use miniature suitcases, which is apparently why Molly bought him one for his birthday (I thought at the time what a curious gift it was.)

In the little suitcase, Brad carried a hand towel, complete with name-tag, a small bottle of pop and a little plastic box containing his 'lunch', which comprised a piece of fruit or a carrot, a cupcake and two or three biscuits or some crisps. And as his little towel stayed at school all week (until Friday when it came home for washing) the meagre contents rattled around in the case like four dried peas in an empty saucepan.

As things progressed, the case included a plastic bag to protect any book which he was asked to bring home. Homework for a four-year-old? In those days it was unheard of.

Evenings were long as we had no television, but we'd often entertain ourselves by switching out the lights, opening the curtains and watching a storm. Our night guard must have thought we were nuts.

One night there was an almighty fizzling flash as lightning struck very close by. Before I'd even taken a step, there was such a loud BOOM of thunder that not only the windows, but the entire house shook. I don't know how, but Ziggy slept right through it.

But then he could sleep on a clothes line in the middle of a battlefield. Why on earth there should be a clothes line in the middle of a battlefield, I really don't know.

Ziggy had commented (before he fell asleep in the chair) that whilst there were plenty of storms around, they always seemed to be on the horizon. Famous last words.

A few minutes later it started to rain so I decided I'd better check on the windows.

I don't recall mentioning when I described the house that it had no gutters or drainpipes. Instead, the roof had a considerable overhang so when it rained the water poured straight off the roof and landed in a shallow concrete channel which surrounded the building.

The point of enthralling you with such riveting detail, is that because of the roof overhang, we didn't need to close the windows when it rained. At least that was the theory, which we trusted obediently, until one week when we experienced a terrible rain storm.

The wind was so ferocious it was lashing the rain against the windows and I suddenly realised I had better go and close them. That was quicker said than done, as each one was opened and closed by a handle which had to be turned, like the window on a car.

Once I'd shut the windows in the lounge and our bedroom and made it as far as Brad's bedroom, there were huge pools beneath his two open windows and water was pouring off the curtains more akin to the shower curtain in the bathroom.

I didn't know what these curtains were made of but the water streaming off them looked remarkably like Guinness. The wall beneath the curtains – originally brilliant white – was now a streaky, shitty-brown colour. After another window closing exercise I eventually cleared up the mess with cloths and bucket and made my way back to the lounge, only to see water coming under the front door and seeping in through the sides of the window frame next to it. After attending to that I stood guard with a bucket and mop until the storm abated.

Talking of things brown reminded me of Christmas, more specifically mince pies.

Mince pies were some of the things I realised we would have to do without, as I hadn't seen any sign of mincemeat on the supermarket shelves. Crackers were another, though most of the time in the past we used to forget to put them on the table anyway. Talking of crackers, neither had I seen any cream crackers since I'd been there, but as there was no cheese to have with them it was pretty immaterial.

Then I saw a notice in the post office saying it was two days before the last post to the UK could be guaranteed to arrive for Christmas. This threw me into a panic of writing Christmas cards. Of course, I couldn't just put 'Love from Ann, Ziggy and family'.

When sending cards to folk I had not got around to writing letters to yet, I felt obliged to put more than just a few words on the back. And there were

52 cards!! Christmas cards are not the sort of things you can easily wind through a typewriter. Talk about writers' cramp...

It also didn't feel at all Christmassy. Daily temperatures bordering 30°C had a lot to do with it. By the end of November the UK shops would have been draped with yards of bright tinsel and giant baubles, and the streets in the centre of my home town would have been ablaze with lights flashing in the festive forms of holly, candles, bells and Santas.

There were absolutely no decorations adorning the streets or in the shops. Well, there weren't in Kitwe. I was told they had some in Chililabombwe, some 50 miles away, but that was rather a long way to go just to get in the mood, as it were.

One morning I decided to call the telephone exchange to try to book a call to my folks on Christmas Day. The operator said the earliest he could do it would be 11:15 – at night, (9:15pm UK time) so I thought I'd better leave it until I could find out where my parents were likely to be at that time of night.

After I'd put the phone down and had a think, I realised that if bookings had already been filled almost to midnight, if I didn't organise it there and then, I probably wouldn't be able to register a call for Christmas Day at all. So I got through to the operator again. It was a different operator. The conversation went something like this:

"I'd like to book a call to England on Christmas Day."

"What time do you want to make the call?"

Hoping for a better response than before, I said

"Well, it would be great if I could book it for the morning, but any time will do really."

"What is the number?"

"That depends on what time you can put me through."

"Oh, anytime tomorrow?"

"No, I want to make the call on Christmas Day."

The operator disappeared for about five minutes, then came back.

"Christmas call bookings are only being taken from the 20th December onwards."

I bade him farewell.

Goodness knows what the first guy had been talking about, he was probably going to connect me that night, which would not have been good as the cost of calls to the UK were exorbitant.

I made mention of our night guard earlier, but think I should enlarge upon the subject.

Guards were essential for security - especially at night - against roaming robbers, not loitering lions.

They were supplied by Rhinestone and changed shifts at six o'clock every day. Although we didn't always get a day-guard, it was quite useful to have one as the gate was always locked from the inside, so if we all went out we needed someone to unlock the gate when we got back.

They just sat, usually under the carport, for 12 hours doing absolutely nothing – other than opening the gates when required. You never saw them reading a book or trying to occupy their time with anything. You would think they'd be bored out of their minds, but I was told the word 'boredom' didn't exist in the Zambian vocabulary.

Talking of words, maybe I should explain another thing.

If you wanted a worker of any description to do something, you had to be extremely specific with regard to the timing. For example if you said, "Can you do such-and-such for me," a worker would assume that meant 'sometime this week'.

If you said, "Can you do this 'Now'?" the interpretation progressed to 'today if possible'.

"Now Now" would be some time during the next hour.

"Now Now Now" advances to 'do this *immediately*'.

The slow pace of Zambia was still taking quite some getting used to.

16

November 1980
Hello All,

Sorry I haven't written to you for so long — it must be almost two weeks, but what else would you expect? I had other things on my mind, like the sacking of Foster. Enough was enough.

He was accumulating such a collection of little niggles and not-quite-good-enough's that I was up to here ↑(just above my eyebrows) with him by lunchtime.

As I've said before, his washing of clothes left a lot to be desired, but the other day I had to pick out three of Brad's T-shirts before I could find one clean enough for him to wear to school. Not to mention Vicki's dresses. And socks are even worse.

I know my lot can get filthy on the best of days, but it doesn't mean they must begin the day wearing dirty clothes.

One morning I was about to start compiling a verse to put in my Dad's birthday card, when I spotted Foster gradually sweeping his way towards the lounge. I didn't want to be disturbed once I started typing (needed to concentrate, you know) so went and asked him to sweep the lounge floor now.

To give him space to work, I took the kids down to Brad's bedroom and played with them there for a good 10 minutes. Ample time, you would think, to sweep one floor. When I got back, Foster had gone, so I took up position at the typewriter, ready to give it my best shot.

I happened to glance down and noticed 'bits' on the floor by my feet. I looked around some more and there were 'bits' all over the place.

Sod me, I'd just wasted ten minutes keeping out of his way and he still hadn't done what I asked. I went into the kitchen.

"Foster, could you please come and do the floor now-now, because I want to get on with my work."

He followed me through to the lounge – carrying a duster! I thought, *I don't believe this.*

"Foster, do you understand what I want you to do?"

Foster just stood there with a stupid look on his face.

"Sweep the floor," I said again, doing my best charades. "You know, like with a brush!"

He grinned broadly and announced, "Yes, Madam, I have done that already."

I gave up, muttering under my breath, "You could have bloody well fooled me."

And I had believed that the floors were his speciality. *Forget it.*

Then there was the food. It was agreed when he was initially employed that he would get a certain amount of food each working day. I would always slice a couple more pieces of bread than we needed in the morning, so he could have toast for his breakfast. At lunch time I would do extra vegetables, so there were always some left in the serving dishes for him. Not scraps from the plates you understand, the dogs had those. I even let him take the carcass if we had chicken – which I would normally have kept for making soup.

I was assured by those who know about these things, that in the event of no leftovers, to offer a boiled egg and a tomato for lunch was quite acceptable. We also provided all his mealie meal.

Mealie meal was the staple diet of 98% of the local population. A powder, similar in appearance to semolina, was cooked in a big pot with water, until it resembled a sort of gooey porridge. The cooked form looked like sticky mashed potato, but it did not taste anything like mashed potato. In fact, from what I could gather (never having the desire to try it myself) it didn't taste of anything much at all, apart from whatever you served with it.

Mealie meal, or *nshima* as the cooked substance is called, also made up the bulk of the dogs' meals in the absence of Winalot dog biscuits. So we bought it by the 50 kilogram sackful, which Foster kept in the *kaya* and from which he topped up our supply for the dogs as and when necessary.

One day Foster came to me.

"Ah, Madam, I am sorry."

I looked at him and waited for him to tell me what he was sorry for. Nothing. I looked him in the eye/s and raised my eyebrows, prompting him to tell me what he was sorry about.

"I am sorry, Madam, I have no tea."

I looked at him for a while, trying to figure out what he was talking about, but eventually shook my head and gave up.

"Foster," I said, "I didn't ask for any tea."

"Ha, ha. No, Madam," he chuckled, "*I* have no tea."

I waited.

"I was wondering, Madam, if the Madam could give me some of her tea?"

I nodded in understanding. "Now I see. You want me to give you some of *my* tea."

"Yes, Madam," he said with a half-toothless grin, "the Madam is very kind."

The Madam hasn't agreed to it yet, I thought.

"Okay, Foster. You may have some of my tea." Whereupon I put about eight teaspoons of my precious PG Tips into a cup.

"Here you go Foster, bring the cup back now."

Foster backed out of the kitchen amidst profuse thankyous, carrying his tea like it was a precious religious idol.

In the days which followed, it continued: *I have no cooking oil.* Given that when it appears in the shops it comes in 5 litre cans, which he would be unlikely to afford, I gave him some of that too.

Then it was, "I have no salt."

I wasn't happy about him coming asking for stuff so frequently, but let it pass until I'd had chance to discuss it with Molly.

But it got worse, because after that he didn't bother to ask for those things, he just helped himself. Although to give him his due, he didn't sneak it, he was quite happy just to help himself even if I was in the kitchen. I was getting a bit peed-off with this and mentioned it to Ziggy.

Then one lunch time we'd had something with chips, plus bread and butter. When the meal was over I told Foster he could have the left-over chips and veg, and even pointed out the appropriate dishes in case he didn't understand me (not unusual).

That night Ziggy and I decided to have sandwiches for supper. Well, that was the plan, but we couldn't find the loaf of bread.

We searched every shelf of the fridge and every cupboard in the kitchen, including the ones containing bleach and shoe polish just to be sure, but alas, no bread. We had omelette instead.

The next morning Ziggy pounced on Foster immediately as he entered the kitchen and asked him if he had taken the bread. He simply said, "Yes."

Ziggy told him he was taking too many things without asking permission and he was not to do it in future. However his requests for things continued, as did my lack of patience.

At the time of the ticking-off, Ziggy also reminded Foster that it was his job to go around and clean up after the dogs; ie. shovel up all the dog muck, dig a hole somewhere in the garden and bury it.

By Thursday we were still hopping over the same dollops of dog poop. Foster had done nothing about it. I wasn't too surprised, as I had told him on several occasions that it needed to be done on a daily basis, but to no avail.

I think the only time he did clear it up without being reminded, was after one of the kids had come sliding into the house announcing, "Look Foster, I've got dog poo on my foot."

The crunch came one Friday morning. I was walking down the steps by the front door and nearly went arse over tit as I slipped on some freshly deposited chicken crap on the second step.

My brain screamed out, *ENOUGH IS ENOUGH. The chickens have to go, and so does he.*

In the afternoon I phoned Molly to find out what our legal obligations were regarding giving Foster the sack and found that as well as this month's wages we had to give him one month's notice, which could be cut short if we gave him one months' money in advance. Unfortunately, we were also bound to give him one month in which to find alternative accommodation.

Not wanting to be the one to break the news to him, I persuaded Ziggy to perform the dastardly deed before he went to work on the following Monday.

Ziggy said he appeared to take it remarkably well and tootled off to the site. A short while later I looked out of the kitchen window to see Foster standing by the *kaya* in a bit of a trance. I shortly discovered it was because he hadn't understood a single word Ziggy had said, and he came to me to clarify the matter.

I felt a complete heel. I kept thinking, 'but his washing-up is alright' and 'his ironing's okay' and 'he seems to be relatively honest'.

But then I thought 'dog shit', 'chicken crap' and 'dirty clothes' and confirmed that he'd just been given the sack. That this was 'the parting of the ways, Sunshine'.

And to make sure he got arse into gear, I said that he could have this month's K50 wages and next month's severance pay as soon as he moved out.

Now he understood that alright, because on Tuesday lunchtime he announced that he had found somewhere else to live and only had one more load of his belongings to remove. So I arranged for him to collect his pay on Wednesday – and he understood that easily enough, too.

It's funny how the one thing that caused many of the problems - his lack of understanding of English - seemed to disappear during any conversation about money.

However his happiness at this unexpected windfall coming his way evaporated rapidly on the Wednesday morning, when he discovered that out of his vast pay-off he must refund to us the K40 loan we had advanced to him the month before.

As they say in other foreign places, *c'est la vie*. That's life!

10th December 1980
Dear Pat,
    This is the first opportunity (or read 'energy') that
I've had to reply to your last letter. What was it you
said about me being a 'lady of leisure'?
    "Nothing to do all day but laze around?", "Waited on
hand and foot?"?
    Balderdash!! We recently sacked our house servant and
since then I have been grafting my arse off.
    I am seriously beginning to doubt the wisdom of having
this 'Big House', with 9½ rooms and three miles of
corridors. And having the bedrooms on the ground floor
means they get much more traffic than if those rooms were
upstairs, especially as that is where the toys are
supposed to be kept.

I then enlarged upon the extent of these household chores to my old school
pal, something along these lines:

The Floors

Before I could sweep the floors, I had to make the beds. And before I
could make the beds, I had to sweep the sheets. Yes, I did say sweep the
sheets.

With all the dust, sand and grit being traipsed in by a tumultuous number
of feet each day, a substantial amount of this debris got transferred to the
beds.

I had mounds of sweepings the size of molehills every morning. I was
surprised there was any earth left in the garden.

Then came …

The Washing

You may by now have gathered that there were no washing machines.
Any allusion to a Bembamatic referred to a member of the Bemba people
using the bath for the purpose of washing everything. (Bembas were the
primary clan of the Copperbelt region.)

Fortunately, we were considerably luckier than most as the scullery
beside the kitchen housed a utility sink. This was a large, squarish, stone sink
where the front section sloped towards you and had a ribbed effect like an
old-fashioned wash-board. Much less back-breaking than using the bath,
making the laundry chore so much easier.

It didn't seem very damned easy to me!

The local washing powder was designed for cold water and according to manufacturers' instructions which I diligently read, you simply soaked the clothes, shook them about a bit and hey presto clean.

Ha, bloody ha!

Whoever wrote out those instructions lived in Cloud Cuckoo Land or didn't have kids.

So, after the soaking, I then resorted to a bar of hand soap and a shoe brush (no, not the one we used for the shoes) to remove those famous stubborn stains. This could take up to an hour or so, until the water had turned quite warm from the sweat dripping off my brow.

But it was more than I dare do to leave the slightest sign of dirt on anything, as I had just sacked someone for doing just that!

Then it was rinse/wring/repeat three times, soak in fabric softener, wring, then spend the next half hour hanging it all out on the line. I was amazed that we could get fabric softener, given the trouble we had finding washing powder most of the time.

The nearest one came to a tumble dryer was if the laundry basket was dropped on the way to the washing-line and then the whole lot went tumbling down the drive.

The Ironing

Now, we're not talking 'ironing to remove the wrinkles' here, but severe ironing to get rid of the putzi fly larvae which I mentioned earlier.

I knew this had to be taken seriously after a report from Steve and Jan. Apparently Steve had developed a small spot on his back, but as it got bigger and redder they realised it was no ordinary spot. About three or four days later it resembled a large boil and when the head formed they 'popped' it, and sure as eggs is eggs a big fat maggot wriggled out. URGH.

So a proper job of the ironing was essential.

Other Stuff

Apart from cooking most of the meals, this now had to be followed by doing all the washing up involved in the preparing and eating thereof. And of course bathroom cleaning was a must. But as for chores like dusting... well, I didn't notice much dust.

Finally do not forget...

The Dogs

Each morning, I removed two packets of frozen pet food from the freezer and left them to thaw in a plastic container.

This procedure could not be accomplished overnight or you would walk into the kitchen the next day to a frenzied fog of big black flies which I can assure you can detect the odour of thawing chicken gizzards from a distance of forty kilometres.

Once thawed it had to be cooked, with cabbage added for flavour.

We had already learned the mistake (via Foster) of cooking this in an open pot in the kitchen. The stench was enough to make even those with the strongest of constitutions throw up over an area of several yards.

Whilst we used to make Foster cook this revolting concoction out in the garden, I avoided going to that extreme. You see I knew I could trust myself to use the pressure cooker without blowing up the house. This method of cooking reduced the obnoxious odours considerably.

Then the mealie meal needed preparing before being combined with the chicken gunge and split into two portions. The first was served for breakfast (TO THE DOGS!!!!) and the remainder was containerised and kept in the fridge for their supper.

One did not prepare more than one day's worth at a time, as even containerised and stored in the fridge, it would likely procreate and take over the kitchen in no time at all, like some sci-fi slime creature. Actually just writing about this is making me feel quite nauseous.

With or without all the graft, I was far from bored with life in Zambia. Since we arrived I had played tennis, badminton and attempted rowing. We'd been to a cricket match and boxing tournament, both international, and had become involved with the local Little Theatre.

It would be fair to say that we had more variety in our lives in the first three months than in the previous three years in Burton.

During one of my 'spare' moments, I managed to look around a couple of shops in Kitwe that professed to sell toys and things, to see what treasures they had to offer for the kids' Christmas presents. It pretty much amounted to the square root of bugger-all.

We had been invited to spend Christmas Day with a couple called Sheila and Graham. We didn't know them very well, but apparently they had this wonderful penchant for helping newcomers to 'settle in'.

It seemed it was the done thing here for a batch of couples to get together for Christmas, thus sharing the cost and difficulty of obtaining the appropriate Christmas fare.

One Wednesday we had a meeting of 'The Ladies' to see what had to be done by whom. In the absence of any obliging turkeys, each family had to provide a cooked chicken, then the purchase and preparation of the remaining fare was distributed mostly according to who knew where to buy it. I offered to provide enough home-made bread sauce for everyone, which if I do say so myself, I am pretty hot at. This was so well received that I was excused making anything else. It was all very well organised.

Apart from one couple, all the husbands were Rhinestone employees, so we already know most of them, even if only a little. I must admit that at first I thought I'd prefer us to spend Christmas day at home, but then couldn't think how it would be much different to any other day. Once I found out more about it, the new plan seemed a far superior idea. I particularly liked the novelty of being able to go swimming on Christmas Day as Sheila and Graham had a pool. I knew the kids would love it.

There were to be 14 adults and 6 children and I had no idea where we would all sit for the meal.

83

As well as all the chores I was now doing I needed to make a start on some sewing. In particular I had to make a shirt for Brad ready for the dress rehearsal of the school Christmas concert.

Brad was to be 'Jack' of 'Jack and Jill' fame. The school were actually putting on a nativity play, but those too young to take part in that were to play the characters of various Nursery Rhymes.

We thought the teachers did well to cast Brad in this part, as he seemed to be spending a lot of his time falling down at home as he performed his impersonation of the Muppets' Fozzie Bear routines.

Greeting inside the Christmas card to Nancy, Mev and Doris:
To be opened only on Christmas Day.

Good Morning, Merry Christmas. May the three of you enjoy
A day that's full of merriment, a year that's full of Joy

That you are there, and we are here may not be very funny
But think of all the better points - you should save lots of money.

Your petrol bills must now be halved, your trips to Winshill fewer.
Your sherry orders cut right down, of that we can be shewer (sure -sorry!)

And over here, we think of you quite frequently, I'll tell you
And now, as Christmas Day arrives we definitely will do.

We'll miss the midday panic trying to get the dinner ready
Prawn cocktails, Turkey, Christmas Pud - and Doris, none too steady!

And after lunch, the great collapse when everyone recovers
On beds, settees and easy chairs, from kids to great-grandmothers.

At night was when the 'riff-raff' came, the folks whose names escape us
They'd eat our grub and drink our booze and then, at cards, they'd paste us.

Alas, on Christmas Day this year we cannot be together
But then, our consolation is at least we've got good weather!

The Christmas decorations will be hanging from the ceiling
We hope the Christmas tree will give our house a festive feeling.

The presents round the Christmas tree may not be all that many.
To send them out, or buy them here does cost a pretty penny.

And so, this year, we'll send to you our greetings on this paper
Although, to choose some fitting words is really quite a caper.

We wish we could be there with you to celebrate, as normal
But no, we will not dwell on that - It makes the verse too formal.

I'll just attempt to end this ode in words that are quite cheerful
We wouldn't want your Christmas Day to start off very tearful.

So,

A Merry Christmas, One and All and as this year is ending
Good Luck, Good Health, and most of all, our love to you we're sending.

XXXXX

December 1980
Dear All,
   It seems ages since I wrote a letter to you. On checking, it actually is.
   I did send other stuff, but that was verses for birthdays and Christmas. So now I have to back-track a bit.
   In early December a bloke pitched up at the gate asking if we needed a gardener. Someone else had been trying to put us in touch with a houseboy who also cooked and if we employed him, we would also need a gardener as a cook/houseboy would hardly have time to do the garden as well as everything else.
   The gardener seemed to have good references, so I said I would keep him in mind and instructed him to call back later in the week. The following day another chap arrived at the gate to say he was looking for a job as houseboy (we had put the word out). He also came with good references but couldn't cook, so I said I'd let him know, wanting to give first option to one who could.
   Shortly thereafter, I found Leon making some very interesting mud pies — out of dog poo! The next time the gardener bloke appeared I instantly gave him a job, on a paid-by-the-week basis until we sorted out the houseboy issue.
   His name was Boneface! (pronounced Bonnyface). Could you picture me shouting "Boneface!" from the kitchen door when I needed to specify his daily chores?

We soon realised that the cooking houseboy wasn't going to materialise, so we decided to employ the uncooking one. His name was Hollins.

   I could not understand why the Zambian people have such peculiar names, and we ARE talking first names here. I would have expected more traditional African names.

   When I asked the question of one of the older expatriates she said that years ago the servants would often name their children after the surname of their employer. I could go with that up to a point,

   "But what happened if they had more than one child?" I asked. "From what I've heard, some houseboys stay with a family for decades. And from what I've seen they have loads of kids too. They can't call them all by the same surname!"

"No," she replied, "then they find something else, like the farm tractor or the bwana's car."

I thought, *there must be a helluva lot of Masseys, Fergusons, John Deeres and Fords around.*

"OR," she'd continued, "the mother may name the baby after an event or a feeling, or even something she saw around the time of the birth."

I didn't know how true any of this was, but it seemed to make a modicum of sense to me at the time.

I was chatting to Ziggy later and mentioned this phenomenon.

"Baby, you ain't heard nothing yet." he sang.

"Our tea-boy at the site office is called Poison!"

It certainly makes you wonder what the mother was thinking of after she gave birth to *that* one.

But I digress again.

I had made a point of telling Hollins all about Foster's shortcomings, so that he knew right from the start that he wouldn't get away with such doings. He sounded okay.

He offered to learn to cook, and to babysit when required. He even offered to take Ziggy to show him where he lived. He said he was currently employed by a Greek couple, but wasn't happy there, as they 'treated him like rubbish'. He said he would have to give ten days' notice, but as it turned out, his current employers insisted he work four weeks. Hollins announced he would report for duty on Monday the 30th December. That confused me somewhat, as Monday was the 29th.

In the event, he didn't turn up on either day.

Christmas Eve had been a bit of a disaster. I had no transport so was stuck at home. Then there was the most amazing lightning storm, so I wasted a lot of time watching that.

As the day wore on, it got worse. The day, not the storm.

Ziggy came home in the early afternoon. He was feeling very depressed. I couldn't remember seeing him like that since we'd arrived in Zambia, or ever if it came to that. Apparently after he'd finished work at lunchtime he went into town to buy a Christmas present for me. As he roamed from shop to shop he found what I had discovered weeks earlier, that there was nothing worth buying.

He is normally quite extravagant, especially when it comes to buying gifts. When he found nothing at all, it really got him down. So he came home and cursed about Zambia and all its pitfalls which, until this point, he'd passed off as being 'just one of those things we have to accept'.

We spent the rest of the afternoon consoling each other until evening was upon us, when we put the kids to bed amidst great excitement that Santa Claus would visit whilst they were sleeping.

I still had a million and a half things to do, but truly could not whip up the enthusiasm. At about a quarter to eight I said to Ziggy,

"I wish I had the time to go to this carolling do at the Theatre Club. It would be my one last chance of trying to get into the spirit of Christmas."

He replied that there was nothing so urgent or important to do at home and that if I wanted to go, then GO. So I did.

As I arrived at the theatre I encountered some confusion because the man who had originally organised this little event had been involved in a road accident so was unable to make it.

By 8:30 someone had found and handed out the song sheets and I sat at the bar surrounded by friends and sang my heart out. To round it off, when the masses dwindled, a few of us stayed at the piano and with Keith Pickersgill, our local impresario, tickling the keys, we set about having a good old sing-song.

We started off with Beatles oldies, but finished up with the old classics – Daisy, Daisy, My Old Man Said Follow The Van, It's A Long Way To Tipparary, etc. etc. So many of the old war-time songs I had learned from my parents when I was a little snot-rag the age of Brad. My grandmother Doris would have *loved it.*

When I arrived home Ziggy was also in much better spirits. (I think he'd been partaking of some, actually.)

The solitary bell on one of the Christmas tree boughs tinkled as a light breeze wafted in through a partially opened window. Suddenly the tree lights seemed to be twinkling a bit brighter than before, reflecting off the yards of tinsel.

We agreed that maybe it wasn't such a bad thing to have had a poor 'eve', as it meant Christmas day could only get better.

Then we stacked the paltry presents under the tree, dimmed the lights and buggered off to bed.

CHRISTMAS 1980

Predictably, Vicki was the first up. As soon as I heard her moving around, I had to shift myself to make sure she didn't wander into the living area. I managed to keep her occupied for half an hour before the two lazy-bones (three if you count Ziggy) had got out of bed. During that time Vicki had said nothing about Santa.

The instant Leon appeared he said, "Santa's coming while I've been asleep, isn't he?" (He has a lovely way with words.)

And so Christmas began.

Ziggy and I took ourselves into the kitchen, to watch proceedings through the 'secrecy' of the hatch and told the kids to go into the lounge.

In total silence they stood and looked at the presents spread out under the Christmas tree.

Eventually I called from the kitchen, "Has anyone been here in the night?"

To which an excited chorus erupted, "Santa!"

We sat around with our cups of tea and NO shortbread. I could not believe it. Shortbread was our traditional Christmas morning fare and was the one thing I *did* have the ingredients for, but I had forgotten to make it.

To have the presents look more plentiful, I had wrapped everything individually. Lollypops, tubes of boiled sweets (like hole-less Polofruits), crayons, colouring books, school exercise books, pencil sharpeners, and sugar coated peanuts. Of course I didn't wrap each crayon, sweetie or peanut separately, but you know what I mean.

There were shirts for the boys and a dress for Vicki, all of which I'd managed to make at the last minute. And a pencil case for each child made from the same fabric as their bedroom curtains (now a few inches shorter), so they couldn't fall out over which belonged to whom.

Whilst Brad and Vicki made no big deal out of opening their presents, Leon in his inimitable style, really slayed us.

"Wow, I've got a BOOK."

"Oh, look! SWEETS!"

"Ooo, a LOLLYPOP!"

You would think he was unwrapping something *really* special, as opposed to the same pathetic junk which he'd been getting for the past four months.

But the best was when he was trying to unwrap his pencil case. He struggled to get it out of the paper and in exasperation, cried, "Mummy, HELP ME, I can't get this bloody curtain out!"

(That was the start of his 'bloody' stage, but we won't go into that right now.)

My only present from Ziggy was the latest publication of the UK Sunday Times. Now I could see why he was so depressed. It didn't do much for me either!

My gift to him was no better. I had actually purchased a pair of shorts for him from a local shop, and when he came to try them on the zip broke!

Shortly after this our booked phone call to the UK came through. It was lovely to talk to everyone, and considering this was the first Christmas we had not spent all together I thought we managed extremely well not to bawl our eyes out on the phone.

At 11:30 we pushed off to Sheila and Graham's place.

Unusually for us, we were among the first to arrive and enjoyed watching the warm welcomes and Christmas spirit which was to stay with us throughout the day.

We sat down to lunch at about three o'clock. Given the limited resources, it was excellent. The menu comprised potato and leek soup, chicken liver pate, roast chickens with all the usual accompaniments, including the normally illusive Brussels sprouts. I didn't know who managed to source those, or from where, but they were greatly appreciated. The feast culminated with Christmas pud and brandy sauce. And the wine flowed freely, and it was not the normal brake fluid variety either!

There were 23 of us in total and the six smaller children had a table to themselves, allowing the rest of us great peace.

And for the first Christmas Day I can remember, we didn't fall asleep after the meal (thankfully, as it would have been terribly rude in someone else's house, in the company of people we barely knew).

Ziggy and the kids thoroughly enjoyed their Christmas Day swim. We eventually left close on midnight. It was amazing that our children had gone all through the day without taking a nap (apart from Leon falling asleep at the table just before lunch was served).

What a day!

Boxing Day arrived far too quickly, mostly thanks to Vicki, who was up at 7:00 as usual. Things then had to happen rapidly.

At Ziggy's behest our Polish egg/chicken man had come up with a goose for us for Christmas, but we felt it inappropriate to take it to the communal do, so kept it for Boxing Day. We had invited Margaret and her husband Gordon to come and share it with us.

Before they arrived I had to set about tidying the house, as we had left it in an awful state when we went out on Christmas Day.

There was wrapping paper strewn all over the floor; sweets and lollypops were stuck to every conceivable piece of furniture and toys were everywhere. Although the kids had very few gifts compared to the previous year, they certainly managed to spread them about well.

Coke had got hold of the sugar coated peanuts leaving substantial evidence of his theft scattered over the floor.

I also needed to go to Sheila and Graham's to collect stuff we had abandoned when we left their house the night before, and just after I returned home Steve and Jan pitched up. In an enthusiastic moment on Christmas Day we had invited them to come around for a drink, totally forgetting about the goose lunch arrangement.

Ziggy played the attentive host whilst I got on with cooking the goose and accoutrements before our luncheon guests arrived.

Our goose was almost cooked (literally as well as proverbially) when Lou and Ryan with Dennis also arrived for drinks, closely followed by our official guests. I only had enough food to feed us and Margaret and Gordon, so couldn't possibly invite the other five to join in the meal. It really was quite embarrassing.

By the time our spur-of-the-moment guests left and we sat down to eat, our goose was truly cooked. Fortunately Margaret and Gordon believed it was intentional to serve it really crispy.

During the course of conversation of Boxing Day, Margaret and Gordon had offered the services of their houseboy during our state of emergency as, not having children yet themselves, they didn't have much work for him. Given that Hollins hadn't arrived as agreed, I took them up on their offer, and arranged for their houseboy to do some washing for us.

Two days later he arrived at 9:30. His name was Laxon for goodness sakes!

Every time I said his name, laxatives and constipation sprang to mind. I had the devil of a job not to laugh each time I saw him, at the mere thought of someone being named Constipation.

Constipated or not, he managed to do a very good job of the washing and had it all finished and out on the line before midday. I thanked him and gave him K1.50 (about 75p in those days).

When you consider that there was over a weeks' worth of washing, and it all had to be done by hand, that was quite a bargain. I actually felt I should have given him K2, but took into account that he was still being paid by Margaret.

Anyway, he was obviously quite happy with it, as he volunteered to come in the following day (his afternoon off from M & G) to do the ironing. Well, never having been one to look a gift horse in the mouth, I naturally accepted. Damn the expense.

A couple of days after Christmas, whilst working in the kitchen, I could hear all the kids singing jubilantly so I went to check them out. There they stood, all in a row like a troupe of miniature disco dancers, bending their knees, shuffling their feet and swinging their arms about – elbows flapping like demented chickens – singing Jingle Bells up the chimney.

I asked them what they were doing and Vicki said, "Singing Jingle Bells to Branbrand."

I could have understood them singing Jingle Bells up the chimney to Santa Claus, but to their Granddad? Highly amused, I left them to it. Later, it all came to light. They weren't singing up the chimney at all, but to a lovely framed photograph of my mum, dad and Doris which they had posted out to us for Christmas and which was sitting proudly on the mantelpiece!

Later that day Leon spent time bombing through the lounge, dodging most of the furniture, on Brad's bike. He could ride that bike almost as well as Brad. It was amazing how the children had advanced since we arrived in Zambia, as I mentioned in this post-Christmas letter to my family.

It is hard to believe that the twins are still some months away from reaching three. In fact, people are very surprised at the range of their vocabulary and conversational abilities, despite Leon's lisp and his tendency to really gabble on.

Sheila and her two daughters popped round one day to return some things we had been unable to find on Boxing Day. Whilst I was making a pot of tea, Leon kept them riveted for a full five minutes. He told them in great detail about: the dogs in the area which kept him awake last night, but which were really big bad wolves; and about how it MUST NOT rain because he didn't want it to; and how his Nanny was coming to visit on an airplane because she couldn't come in the car; and how that was not his book, but this one was. He went on, and on, and on…

Half of the time nobody could figure out what he was ranting about as he was gabbling so fast. And as he hardly paused for breath, no-one else could get a word in.

Don't anyone DARE say ANYTHING about where he gets all this from!

I must dash off now as I really need to go to the theatre to find costumes for Ziggy and me for the fancy dress party on New Year's Eve.

guess who wrote this linew when his missus was/nt looking-? Yours sincerely,Ziggy..
I am sitting here starving, typing with one finger, and not many mistakes either09(except1) Just poured myself a gin & tonic but still bloody starving —Not much of a Christmas this year The Chrissy decorations came down yesterday -wot a lovely bit of typing-another swig, where,s (grammatical error) my Fat Little Wife? Out

sorting out my fancy dress outfitI suppose. It,s taken me
half an hour to type these lines. Ain't I aSmarty Pants ?
I don8t ½ wish I could type proper like wot she can?
9:30pm. Still starving- but getting better at this here
tytping —typing?- there goes my mouth again. Tonight I,ve
done a rather suberb chicken & beef stew, without using
any curry powder/. The potatoes do have some chilli in
them, but not much. Look out, here,s my Missus.

I am not at all impressed when he butts in on my
typewriter. He could do untold damage!
Anyway, I shall finish now as, having come back with
the fancy dress stuff, I find that I have a couple of
hours work to do on my costume, not to mention what I've
got to do to Ziggy tomorrow (chance would be a fine thing
— not got the time!).
Ta-ta for now,
Love, Me X

Dear Nancy, Mev and Doris,

The New Year's Eve party we arranged to attend was at Pam and Chris's house, just across the vlei from us. This was very strictly fancy-dress only. No fancy-dress, no entry.

Pam has been a wonderful friend to me on numerous occasions, like taking me shopping when Ziggy forgot to send the driver, and even doing some last-minute shopping for me on Christmas Eve. We have also borrowed their houseboy Edward on a couple of occasions, to babysit.

I reckon Pam and Chris are a bit younger than us. She's a school teacher and Chris works for the civils side at Rhinestone. I think they were planning to start a family in the not too distant future, but might be having second thoughts now, after witnessing the antics of our youngsters.

Anyway, where was I? Went off at a bit of a tangent there. Oh yes, the party.

One would think being heavily involved in the theatre's wardrobe department that I could organise costumes for Ziggy and me at the drop of a hat. Not so!

I had a particular green dress in mind for myself, with the intention of us going as Robin Hood and Maid Marion. I thought Ziggy would look a treat in a thigh length tunic, green tights and all the other trimmings. Then some stupid bird in the Cinderella chorus line chose my dress as part of her costume. What a bloody cheek, eh? So like an arrow from a bow, that idea flew out the window.

After that I spent almost three hours searching through the rails and boxes. Could I find anything? I could not.

I wanted us to go as a pair of something, but when I got myself fixed up, there was nothing for Ziggy, or when I got him sorted, there was nothing for me. The problem was, it was intended to make the men look as silly as possible, not a difficult task, especially in Ziggy's case, but one does have to be a bit careful.

At one point I found a Bo-Peep type dress which I quite fancied and then found a second one that would have fit Ziggy. Dead right! Then one of the Ugly Sisters in the panto wasn't happy with the dress 'she' had been allocated, and blatantly nicked the one I'd picked out for Ziggy!

There were several medieval type dresses and a box full of those pointy hats with veils, but these dresses were obviously made for scrawny bints, as the biggest I could find was a 32inch bust. Hardly my size!

On Tuesday morning, the day before New Year's Eve, I went round to the Club again, desperate to find something – *anything* - for us to wear.

Ryan was in the bar as I fetched a drink to sustain me in my searches.

"Why don't you just find him a wig and a bra and put him in one of your own dresses?" he suggested. "You can make his face up, put on some nail polish and he'll go down a treat."

That seemed like a fair suggestion, so I set off and duly found a wig and even a padded bra (with frightening memories of my under-developed teens). That was Ziggy sorted out.

I attacked more boxes in search of something for me and discovered the Eastern costumes. I found a reasonable pair of baggy chiffon pants and matching bolero. A trawl through the material bit-box revealed some fabric with which I could make a yashmak and also use to cover one of my bras. A couple of hours sewing should finish my outfit off nicely.

Ziggy hadn't been at all happy about having to get dressed up, but eventually agreed to go along with it so long as I didn't ask him to pick out his own costume, or to try anything on beforehand.

Once home, I immediately set about serving myself some of Ziggy's special supper and got myself a drink. When I walked into the lounge, I nearly dropped the lot.

There stood Ziggy, as large as life and twice as ludicrous, wearing my chiffon baggy pants and bolero. Priceless!

That did it. I knew exactly what he was going as. Unfortunately, it meant another trip to the wardrobe to find a duplicate outfit, but it was worth it.

After collecting the appropriate bits the next morning, I went home and launched into washing Ziggy's wig. Brad appeared and asked what I was doing and why. When I told him it was for Daddy, he looked at me in the strangest way as if to say, "Oh come on Mummy, who do you think you're kidding?"

I tried to explain it to him by making comparisons with the men who dressed up as ladies in the panto. Then he got the picture, sort of.

The day became very hectic as I frantically sewed Ziggy and myself ready. I also had to make a plateful of scotch eggs as my contribution towards the party snacks. As we still had no houseboy all the clearing and washing up from that exercise, as well as from dinners and teas for the kids, was down to me too.

We had organised for Lou and Ryan to bring Dennis to sleep over at our house so they could share our babysitter. As the New Year's Eve party started at 10:30, we would go to the theatre for a quick drink first.

We were already running late, because the security firm who supplied our night guard had lost their contract with Rhinestone and had turned up out of the blue to remove their guard. This resulted in Ziggy having to whiz around to find a replacement from somewhere. He made it back with another guard 'borrowed' from Rhinestone's offices.

I had brought Ziggy a choice of harem outfits in powder blue or emerald green. He felt the powder blue was more his colour, saying that it matched his eyes. When I went into the bedroom to do his makeup, I was totally overwhelmed by the sight before me. He had already donned his baggy pants, but underneath them he wore his jock strap!

I don't know if you've had any experience of jock straps. In my opinion they are not a pretty sight at the best of times; but exposed beneath sheer, powder blue chiffon… Well, it was just something else, the eye-catcher being the huge bulge at the front and bare arse framed by the narrow straps at the rear..

I really don't know what noises escaped from me at that precise moment, but they must have been raucous. Lou happened to be passing the bedroom door and thought I was being attacked, and I apparently scared the living daylights out of the kids, who had already gone to bed.

Once I'd composed myself and convinced Ziggy that the jock strap route was *not* an option, we decided that since none of his underpants looked right either, he should wear a pair of my knickers. The containing effect wasn't much better than the jock strap, but was immeasurably more respectable, if you can call a man wearing women's knickers respectable.

I adjusted his padded bra and bolero, applied his make-up and clipped the wig, head-dress and veil in place. It was as well I hadn't yet applied my own makeup, as tears of laughter were still streaming down my face, and it was a wonder I could actually see what I was doing.

I then led him out for inspection by Lou and Ryan.

By this time the stupid bugger had got himself well and truly in the mood and sauntered into the lounge, hips swaying, arms floating afore and aloft, talking in a high-pitched voice. Lou and Ryan, dressed conservatively by comparison, as a vicar and tart couple, went into convulsions.

Brad, having heard the shrieking and howling, came to find out what was going on. His face was a picture. He just stood there, eyeing his dad up and down, with a look of absolute disbelief.

Then Ziggy said, in his girlie voice, "Do you know who I am?"

Brad, rolling his eyes heavenward replied,

"Yes, Daddy!" and stomped off to his bedroom in total disgust.

During all this hilarity, we had totally forgotten about Edward (the babysitter) who was also sitting in the lounge.

The locals can be very humble. Edward was normally particularly so. But when I glanced across at him, I could see it was taking the poor sod all his time to keep a respectful straight face, which mingled with an expression of extreme incredulity at the goings-on of these eccentric Englishmen. I was sure we would never tempt him to babysit for us again.

I eventually got myself sorted and we headed off to the Club.

I had intended letting Ziggy walk in first by himself, but was just too selfish to cheat myself from seeing the expressions on people's faces when they caught sight of him, so we all walked in together.

It was classic!

Most people instantly knew who it was chiefly, I think, because I was with him. But they just could not believe that this was the Ziggy they knew, the Boss Man.

The majority of the Rhinestone people who were members of the Club either worked for Ziggy, or alongside him and never dreamt he was capable of such wild abandon.

A white guy who was born in Zambia and was known as 'Blackie', worked for Ziggy. He couldn't believe his eyes. I battled to understand this as Blackie had been a member of the theatre for years and regularly took part in the productions that the Club put on. He was actually one of the Ugly Sisters in that year's panto, for goodness sake, and very good at it too.

"I don't know how you've got the nerve," said Blackie. "It's one thing to get up on stage and play the idiot, but it's another to walk into a bar looking like a total prat!"

Then I saw his point, since we were the only ones in the entire place wearing fancy dress. We quickly finished our drinks and made a hasty retreat.

When we arrived at the party, Ziggy was an instant success. And whilst he didn't win the prize for the most original costume, he did get a special prize for being the funniest. The prize was a toilet roll. Our compatriots have a great sense of humour.

After eating, we moved onto the games. Chris took charge and as self-appointed Chairman of the Games Committee, organised charades.

"Right, men on one team, ladies on the other. And all those who don't want to play have no choice."

Even Ziggy joined in, totally unheard of before.

And so, my dearest Mum, Dad and Nannan, we brought

1980 in Kitwe to a close.

At 12 midnight we sang in our New Year. Then we repeated auld lang syne at 2am to the chimes of Big Ben. Ziggy and I drank a special toast to you three and all the customers who we knew would be celebrating with you at the Burton Arms. At 4am we raised our glasses yet again to someone in another time zone — God knows who or where.

Honesty prevailing, let it be acknowledged that lots of drinking, singing and dancing went on. I must admit that it did feel a bit weird doing smoochy dances with Ziggy - it is not quite the same cuddling a man when you know he is wearing your knickers.

We eventually staggered home accompanied by the rising sun at 6:15, to be met by the day-guard who had just come on duty and who seemed totally impervious to the strange goings-on of these loony expats.

On that note we say Goodbye to 1980. It only remains to wish you a wonderful, marvellously happy, healthy and wealthy 1981.

Love, Me   xxxxxxxxxxxx
          ...plus

BARAD

VIC
          KY

(Leon says) "You know I can't type yet, Mummy"

She let me have the final say, so here it is! Ziggy for President!!

- Last word my backside, in your dreams, Ziggy. In your Dreams!

January 1981
Dear All
 Oh, the luxury, the sheer bliss, the love of my life,
the culinary classic, the truly delectable flavour. I
found cheese!!!!
 You cannot begin to understand how I have missed it.
Long may the supply continue. It is nothing special you
understand, just some ordinary, common or garden cheddar
type stuff, but IT IS CHEESE nonetheless.
 As for the next luxury: I am now back in clover, lying
on a bed of roses (thornless), veiled in velvet, cocooned
in comfort and all that rot. Yes, you've guessed it.
Hollins rocked up for work on the 2nd. I stood in the
dining room in a daze, overwhelmed by the view through
the hatch into the kitchen - of Hollins doing the chores.
 I eventually dragged myself off to put away the
ironing Laxon had completed and as I left each bedroom,
had to control the automatic impulse to make the beds!
This means I can actually enjoy a leisurely weekend.

The leisurely weekend began in the garden, where I lazed on a locally made wicker arm chair, with an upturned packing crate in front of me, on which sat my typewriter.

Ziggy was about 8 feet away braai-ing meat and had just brought me an ice cold beer and one for himself, of course.

Our LP of the Jesus Christ Superstar film soundtrack was blasting out from the lounge and reaching us at an acceptably high volume. I assumed the neighbours were enjoying it too.

The temperature was sitting at 33C (93F) in the shade, it had been 29C at 9:30 that morning. The sun beat down on my shoulders and the kids ran around the garden in their birthday suits. This is the life, I thought.

Talking of the kids, we had only managed to stop Brad calling everyone a 'stupid bugger' just before we left England. You may remember my mentioning that Leon, attempting to open his 'curtain' pencil case on Christmas day, was going through a 'bloody' phase. One morning he came up to me, in a most frustrated manner just after he'd been for a wee.

"I can't get these bloody trousers up," he said.

Later, all three of our offspring were scurrying around the lounge floor. I asked them what they were doing.

"We're just chasing a bloody lizard, Mummy," Leon explained.

I tried very hard not to laugh at these little gems, but it was not easy. Ziggy would get very cross with the kids when he heard them use a little swearword and I'm sure I don't need to tell you who got blamed for it!

After the braai I had to go to the Club for a meeting concerning the costumes for a new production, so I packed away my writing gear and searched out my sewing hat.

My first real involvement in the role of costumier at the Nkana/Kitwe Arts Society came with a play called *The Crucible*. The producer, Paul McDermott, asked me if I would be prepared to 'do costumes'. Thinking he meant just help out, like in previous productions, I stupidly agreed.

Turns out I was to be in charge of organising the whole bloody caboodle and I had to find my own helpers in the sewing capacity. Given that I still hardly knew many people, this was not a good situation to be in, but alas, not one I could back out of.

I soon discovered that there was next to nothing in the wardrobe appropriate to this play, with a cast of twenty-one. It looked like I really had my work cut out (never mind the costumes). The first dress rehearsal was planned for 22nd February, so I set my target for completion to the 14th just to be on the safe side.

The only indication I had of what these costumes were supposed to look like were a few illustrations in an old history book. I had to make skirts, shirts, trousers, jackets and hats, with not a template in sight. As I had not yet tracked down any retailer of buttons meant I could have a serious problem. I mean, how could a city not have buttons?

Paul said he would phone round other theatre companies to see if any of them had put on this play previously and if they had any costumes we could borrow. I didn't know how many active theatres there were in Zambia at the time, but given the dearth of other facilities I would not have expected there to be more than a couple. I truly hoped he succeeded with his endeavours.

I also heard that the play culminated with about half the cast being hanged, though they didn't actually have to act the 'being hanged' bit. I don't mean they did it in reality. Whichever way they did it I just hoped they were very careful or all my work would be a waste of time after the first night.

We had great excitement one day when I went to ZCBC (the main supermarket in Kitwe) and found that they had butter on sale. The queue was only about 25 customers deep, so I duly joined it. Everyone was being allowed a maximum of five slabs. After I left there I called at the Parklands shops and found they were also selling butter. So I got some more! Eleven packets in one day – the exhilaration was almost too much to handle.

The next day I took Ziggy to work so I could have the car, when I spotted people walking around with bags of sugar, so I decided to see where it was coming from, as my stocks were getting quite low. It was ZCBC again. Things were looking up until I saw the queue.

If you can imagine a line of people starting at the bread counter of Sainsburys and snaking the length of the store, out the door and past WH Smith, then round the corner past Boots until you reach Marks and Spencer, then that was the length of the queue. I wasn't *that* desperate for sugar.

But THEN, I noticed a few people with washing powder. Now *that* I was desperate for as we hadn't seen any on the shelves for almost two months. I stopped and asked a lady where she got it from and hotfooted to the relevant shop.

Normally, when someone comes out of a store carrying a 'rare' commodity, thousands of the locals suddenly appear from nowhere like wasps at a picnic and by the time I reach the front of the queue it is all gone. This time there was no queue at all.

You've got it, they were all queuing for sugar!

All except one woman, who I spotted as I was about to drive away. She was obviously intent on not missing out on the washing powder. Anxious to get to the relevant store before the word spread, she was giving it her best speed.

You must understand that I am not being racially derisive, but must say that most of the *chitenge*-clad Zambia ladies had a very distinctive, somewhat unusual way of running.

With the tightly bound *chitenge* fabric clearly constricting their legs, forward propulsion seemed to occur only from the knees down. They would scurry along with the feet swinging out and round like the brushes on a council roadsweeper vehicle, whilst the arms flailed out at each side as if asymmetrically turning two skipping ropes.

As you might imagine, this was quite a spectacle when there were several dozen women executing this manoeuvre, but what this particular performer lost in numbers she certainly made up for in alternative entertainment.

I mentioned earlier that the majority of the women always appeared to have a baby strapped to their backs with a shawl or large towel. This lady had obviously been feeding her child when she got the exciting news about the washing powder, consequently the baby was strapped to her chest.

To put it politely, she was not a small woman. In fact she had breasts the size of water melons and she had obviously not had time – or perhaps she just forgot, or possibly never even intended – to tuck away the current milk dispenser when she commenced her sprint.

The child, probably about seven or eight months of age, was not to be deterred in its endeavours to gain sustenance and as the woman ran, her ginormous breast bounced around before her with the babe frantically trying to catch the generous nipple in its mouth every time the tit swung in his direction. How the mite wasn't knocked unconscious by this weighty appendage I do not know.

I'm sorry, but I laughed until I cried. I just couldn't help it. Thank goodness I was hidden away in the car at the time.

And light upon light, on the following day ZCBC also had SOAP. And not just one, but two brands - Knights Castile and Lux, which were rationed to ten bars. Sadly the trip there wasn't anywhere near so entertaining.

If you looked into our store cupboard at the end of that week it bore a close resemblance to a Tesco warehouse.

23

Dear All,
White Rabbits ... 1st Feb 1981

I forgot to say "White Rabbits" when I woke up this morning. Never mind. When I do remember to say it at the right time, it will be a first.

Ziggy said this morning,"Tell me, why exactly do you say White Rabbits every now and again?"

I cannot believe he has never asked this before, given that I have been doing it since we got married over six years ago. So I explained that on the 1st of each month the very first words you should utter when you wake up are "White Rabbits" — three times. It is supposed to bring you good luck for the rest of the month.

"What a load of rubbish! And you expect ME to do that?" was the response I got.

If you discover my typing to be even more atrocious than usual, it is because the index and middle fingers of my left hand are strapped almost to my wrists in Elastoplast.

I had decided to make some bread. Not knowing how reliable the flour was, I decided to play it safe with rolls rather than a loaf, but I think they got a trifle over-baked. Not surprising really since I had left King Alfred (alias Ziggy) in charge of the oven.

Anyway, I chose to have one of these rolls with my curry, instead of rice. Selecting a lovely sharp knife, I tried to cut it open. The roll was so hard that the knife slipped one way, the roll flew the other way and my fingers got caught somewhere in between. Luckily, it didn't slice my fingers off, but merely took off succulent chunks.

A visit to the Company Clinic next morning easily set them into the healing motion, but when it comes to applying Elastoplast they didn't skimp, so the errant fingers were pretty immobile and quite a hindrance when typing.

On the first Monday in February we were just leaving home to take Brad to school when I had to dash back inside to answer the phone. It was the Headmistress from Brad's school.

My first thought was, *Who has he hit back first this time?* But I did the child an injustice.

On the contrary, as an ambassador of the Patras family he had clearly made a favourable impression because Mrs Forrester announced that she unexpectedly had two vacancies in the Nursery class and wondered if I would be interested in the twins starting early, even though they are not yet three. Would I?

After I had recovered from the shock, I managed to squeak, "Yes, I definitely would be interested!"

"When would you like them to start?"

It took all my willpower not to say, *How about today?*

Breaking my stunned silence she eventually said, "Would they like to come tomorrow?"

I was in shock. After multitudes of 'thank you's and promises of everlasting gratitude, I made my way in a euphoric trance to the car, and told a delighted Vicki and Leon that they would be starting school the next day. They too were thrilled, as they had been eager to go for ages.

We all delivered Brad into the custody of the teacher, mainly so that I could pay personal homage to the Great Sender of Relief and Restorer of Sanity.

Once inside, the Head said, "Well, now they are here you might as well let them *all* stay."

So that's it folks. Vicki and Leon officially started 'school' aged 2 years & 10 months.

With big fat grins on their faces, I left all three Patras juniors in the tender care of the Round Table.

I skipped my way merrily back to the car. Gabriel thought I had really flipped.

Vicki and Leon starting playschool could not have happened at a better time. During the previous week I cut out 23 collars, 23 pairs of cuffs, ten aprons, 12 hats, 11 skirts and 11 blouses. Most of these were delivered to a band of helpers to sew up – except the blouses which I decided to make myself.

I found two very proficient ladies who agreed to make three men's jackets, five jerkins and three pairs of boots. My evenings were taken up with meetings with the producer and to rummaging through the wardrobe in the search of 10 shirts, five capes and two Cleric's robes. But I wasn't complaining. It was the first real challenge I'd had for a long time.

And what a challenge it was, equalled only by one we were having with ticks.

According to those 'in the know' there was a corridor of land probably half a mile or so wide running through Kitwe known as the 'tick belt', which was particularly prone to infestation by ticks, and our McFrazier property was well and truly in it. I used to check the dogs on an almost daily basis for ticks. The big grey ones, plump as M&Ms, were easy to spot but the small brown male ones were the worst as they were close in colour to the dogs' red-setter coats. We would have de-ticking sessions where I would sit with a pair of tweezers and a small dish of pure bleach and scour the dogs for the little blighters. Their favourite areas appeared to be in or on the creases inside the ears, between the shoulder-blades or between their toes. Once traced and removed I would drop them in the dish of bleach and at the end of the session the whole lot would be tipped down the toilet.

Brandy had the biggest problem with ticks mainly because there were so many clumps in her fur it was difficult to find them. I once found a tick latched onto Vicki's back, which I removed with care. Later that day saw Brandy stand up from the corridor floor and walk out. She left behind her a dozen or so tiny brown ticks crawling around on the floor. You couldn't just stamp on them to effect their demise (they are made of leather) and sweeping them up would probably result in half remaining inside the brush. Each one had to be picked up with the tweezers and they were scurrying away in all directions faster than I could catch them. It was horrible.

After that incident Brandy was barred from coming inside. The poor old girl couldn't understand why she was being ostracised.

It reached the point where (oh, I'm getting itchy just thinking about it) I would wake in the middle of the night thinking I had ticks crawling all over me.

One memorable night I awoke in a sweat at about 3am from a dream where I had all the black material for the Crucible laid out on a table, having great difficulties in trying to fit a template on it, only to see ticks crawling all over the paper pattern.

Every time I tried to go back to sleep all I could see were ticks and material, material and patterns, patterns and ticks and so on.

To help solve the problem we got an oil drum, sliced in half like those used for the braai but without the holes. It was wedged in a permanent position near the car port and filled with a solution of tick dip which we managed to buy from the SPCA. The dogs were dipped weekly and that mix was also sprayed around the areas where the dogs most liked to lie. Whilst this didn't eradicate the problem, it certainly lessened it.

Kitwe Little Theatre usually had a film show on a Sunday night, but one week there was a Saturday Special and Ziggy was helping out in the projection room. It wasn't special enough to entice me to watch – *Black Emanuel* (sex film) followed by *Friday the 13th* (gory film). I decided not to bother.

Instead I alternated between chatting to the few people remaining in the bar and taking drinks up to the projection room. The turnout for the film show was pretty good and it occurred to me that having only one barman on duty, the bar would probably get a bit hectic during the interval.

As it happened I had stood a bar duty during the staging of Cinderella, so I knew the prices and location of the various beverages. I offered to help out.

It was a good job I did. Everyone converged on the bar at the same time, tongues hanging out. I wasn't sure if it was a 'thirst' thing or the result of the first movie.

I thoroughly enjoyed myself. It took me back to the good nights at the Burton Arms when we were so busy it felt that a coach-load of people had descended on the pub en masse.

After the interval I wandered up to the back of the theatre and snuck a look at the second film to make sure I wasn't missing anything. I decided I wasn't.

24

February 1981
Dear Nancy,

You are a one! The excitement of your forthcoming visit leapt out of the envelope before I had even opened your last letter. By the time I'd finished reading it I was all of a dither myself. It's a good job the kids can't yet read or they'd be going crazy too.

My fingers are a lot better now, thank you very much if you were wondering. One is completely healed, the other has been downgraded to a sticky-plaster, though still needs to have magic muti (African word for medicine) put on it by the Company Clinic each day to prevent it going septic.

Leon is a scream sometimes. He just came inside and asked me to put his thewths on. I eventually got him to pronounce shoes. But when it came to socks, he could only say thockth. Now he keeps walking into the room saying 'thockth', then leaving as I am responding 'socks'. We are having a running thockth/socks battle.

Talking of things said, Brad came out with a couple of peaches at about this time. He and Ziggy were having a conversation. I didn't catch what about, only the tail-end of it.

Brad said, "That's a silly thing, and Mummy says I am not allowed to do silly things."

Another day he came to me and said, "Mummy, when I keep talking all the time it makes me tired."

"Perhaps you shouldn't talk so much?"

"But I've got to TALK," he responded.

But the absolute classic came from Leon. 'Out of the mouths of babes ...'

Ziggy had organised for two Rhinestone casual labourers to do some work in the garden. I gave one of them a key to the gate so they could dispose of leaves and stuff in the *vlei* across the road. I was standing in the kitchen, Hollins was doing the washing-up and Leon walked in.

Leon: Here you are, Mummy. *(hands me the key to the gate)* This is for you. One of those monkeys in the garden gave it to me.

Me: Thank you, Leon.

I quietly left the kitchen really hoping that Hollins hadn't heard that, but as I turned the corner I could hear him chuckling away at the kitchen sink.

One Tuesday I realised I needed to do something about buying meat and was told that there was usually meat available at a place called Chingola. I thought that was the name of a shop, but found it is a town some fifty kilometres away. Not quite the same as my mum nipping to the butcher twelve doors down the street from the pub.

I asked Gabriel (the Rhinestone driver) to take me to the butcher in Chingola but when we got there they didn't have any meat after all, so I placed an order and arranged to collect it two days later.

On the way back from Chingola we called at a large chicken farm to buy five chickens (dead ones), only to find that the minimum they would sell me was ten. I decided to leave that until I could find someone to share them with as I didn't have room in my freezer for a full flock of chickens.

Later that day I was at the Club and asked Glyn if he wanted any. He agreed to take five. Another bloke was standing at the bar and enquired (several times because I couldn't understand a bloody word he was saying) where I was getting them from.

His name was Nandy and was originally from Hungary. As if trying to get through that accent wasn't bad enough, he had recently had a laryngectomy and was still learning how to speak again.

Anyway, when I told him I was going to get them from 'Peak Chickens' that we had passed en route to Chingola he said,

"In that case, get fifty. Mention my name to a chap named Jim Geitch and you'll get them cheaper. Then I'll take 40 from you."

I arranged to call at his house the next morning to get some money from him.

On arriving at Nandy's it became glaringly obvious that we could have difficulty fitting the driver, myself, my Chingola meat order and 50 chickens plus Nandy (because he had decided to come with us) in the car.

Nandy helpfully offered to take me in his Land Cruiser instead.

The fact that his vehicle was equipped with a tape player swung the decision as I had found the drive to Chingola very boring and it could take anything from forty-five to sixty minutes.

It was only when we were halfway there that it dawned on me that I was being driven into the remote Zambian countryside by a bloke I didn't know from a bar of soap. But I figured that as a lot of folk in the theatre's bar were friendly with him, he must be kosher.

When we got to the butchers they had still only managed to fill half my order. We made a quick detour to a shop Glyn had told me about, to buy him ten trouser zips (he must have a lot of broken trousers) then headed for home, stopping at the chicken farm on the way back.

It transpired Nandy used to work there and remained very pally with Jim the owner who cordially invited us into his house for a very welcome cold beer.

During the course of conversation on the journey I had discovered that

Nandy did a fair amount of catering. He owned two or three take-away kiosks where they sold pies and various other comestibles. He was also renowned as being the best biltong maker on the Copperbelt.

Biltong is dried strips of spiced-up meat, usually beef, and is very popular in Africa.

When we returned to Nandy's house he had two guys there slicing up tons of beef (and throwing it into a bath) for his biltong trade and another bloke making 130 Cornish pasties, so it was obviously not that small an enterprise.

Nandy commented that I was paying far too much for my meat and that the next time I wanted any I was to see him and he would organise it for me. He also sold me a tray of eggs.

That might not sound too egg-citing (sorry) but I had not managed to get any for a week, as my egg man had been sold a load of bad feed and his hens weren't laying. Apparently the same duff feed had been sold to half of the egg growers in the Kitwe area, so there was a general shortage.

That was when I discovered how much it helped to have friends in the right places.

One day I decided that my hair was getting a bit long at the front. Not wishing to trust my long, brown, wavy tresses to a local hairdresser, I chose to trim it myself. Vicki and Leon were watching me and asked to have a haircut too. As theirs wasn't very long I just trimmed their fringes.

When we sat at the dinner table I thought Vicki's hair looked a bit odd, but really didn't pay it much attention. After he'd finished eating, Ziggy went to get washed up ready to go back to work and returned from the bathroom clutching a clump of blond hair,

"What's this?" he asked.

Not being a particularly observant sort of person, when I'd looked at Vicki I'd assumed she'd been playing in water and had swept her hair behind her ear. As it turned out, it's a wonder she had an ear left.

Apparently she decided I hadn't cut her hair short enough and cut it herself – to within half an inch of her scalp. To say she'd had a close shave with a pair of scissors was an understatement.

I couldn't possibly leave it like that, so had to cut the other side to match. I still wasn't happy with it the next day so I cut the lot down to about two inches long all over, removing nearly all her soft blond curls.

The trouble was that from the back Vicki then looked more like a boy making Leon look like the girl twin, so I had to cut his hair short as well. I resolved to restrict my future hair trimming activities to when the kids were not around.

25

February 1981
Dear Mev and Doris,
*   First of all, multitudes of apologies for the delay in*
writing.
*   Secondly, I am sure you will understand if you don't*
hear from me for several weeks after this. It is because
we fully intend to give our undivided attention to Nancy
during her three week visit. By the time you receive this
letter she will hopefully have arrived safely.
*   The reason for the current delay in writing is that I*
have been up to my armpits — and those of other people to
be more precise — in sewing for the past two weeks.
*   I think, and I use these words cautiously, that I may*
now have finished everything for the Crucible play.
*   This afternoon Brad and I sat outside painting the*
turn-back flaps on a pair of boots. I think we got more
paint on ourselves than on the boots.
*   The boots are not boots as such but rather are*
suitably formed, sewn-up pieces of vinyl upholstery
fabric, which creates an extension from a shoe up to the
knee of the person wearing them. And since the inside of
this vinyl stuff is whitish, the turn-downs needed to be
painted black.
*   DO I MAKE MYSELF PERFECTLY CLEAR?*
*   Good.*

During one of the costume checks at the theatre recently I had sent someone
through from the wardrobe to the stage, when I heard a cry.

"What a bloody awful mess. Get off my stage!"

Given the work that I, and others, had put into it I could have cheerfully
strangled the producer. And I was having trouble with *thockth*.

Some of the cast, who weren't important enough to wear boots, were to
wear socks. Black ones. I had no idea why, but black knee length socks were
not readily available in darkest Africa. So I asked the producer if he would
settle for white, due to my inability to find black ones. BIG mistake.

He crapped on me from a dizzy height.

"I gave *you* the job as head of costumes, it's up to *you* to find the
solution."

Since the floor didn't want to open up and swallow me, I had to crawl off to the nearest hiding place.

It was then that I realised what a really good producer he was. He did his bit and expected everyone else to do theirs. And he was the director too, so he had enough on his plate beyond worrying about black *thockth*. I eventually sourced black socks.

Actually, it was quite refreshing to work with a professional type, as in the previous two productions I'd been involved with, the producers couldn't make up their minds what they wanted, until it was too late to do anything about it properly.

Paul knew exactly what he wanted and you bloody well had to find it.

When I needed to be present at the club one Saturday for a dress rehearsal, Ziggy had gone off to work for a few hours in the morning, but knowing that I had to be there by 2:00 he promised to be home by 1:30.

I figured I'd better get lunch ready early, so that I could eat mine before leaving. Ziggy and the kids could eat after I left.

I prepared the potatoes, put the steak in the oven (not the way I'd normally cook steak, but whatever). I picked the required portion of fresh runner beans from the garden and chopped the leeks, which I was going to braise in butter.

I then went up the road to Margaret's place to collect the last pair of boots she had been working on. Unfortunately I stayed there with the tribe for about an hour, leaving just after noon.

On the walk home the rear wheel on Brad's bike seized up so I had to carry the bloody thing back, and for a small bike it was not lightweight.

When we reached home the steak was burned to a crisp. Two pieces I couldn't get my teeth into, even the dog gave me a very questionable look when I fed it to him.

So I got some small pieces of fillet steak out of the freezer and put them into a bowl of water to thaw out quickly. Whilst waiting for this I decided to sweat the leeks. The leeks burnt.

The electric cooker was very difficult to set down to a simmer.

Not to be deterred, I drained off the fat from the meat tin in order to make some sort of tasty gravy, in which to smother the remaining half-dried-up meat. I'd already strained the potatoes and beans, when I realised I should have saved the liquid to use for the gravy.

So what? I thought. (I also thought a few other things but won't put those into print.) *I'll just use plain water for the gravy.*

So I combined it with the un-burnt meat-juices in the tin and mixed in some flour, then stood horrified as it all went into big lumps. The soddin' stove was *still* set too high. By this time I was proper pissed off.

But I will not be beaten.

"Sod you, gravy," I said into the meat tin, "I can use a sieve to extract the lumps'.

So I added some more thickening to achieve the desired consistency then commenced pouring the gravy from the tin, through the sieve, into a jug.

As the meat tin was hot and the sieve was small, the decanting procedure was taking all my concentration so I didn't notice – until it was dripping off the edge of the worktop – that I was trying to fit a pint of gravy into a half pint jug!

By now it was 1:20 and I hadn't even plated my food, let alone eaten it. And I was supposed to leave for the Club at 1:30.

Miraculously I got there before the duly appointed hour. Given how my day had gone thus far, I was fearful of this final dress rehearsal.

It went like a dream.

With the exception of one or two adjustments, the producer announced that the costumes were PERFECT. I couldn't believe my ears. Finally Saturday had turned into a whopping good day.

That meant that I could stop having nightmares.

Dreams of people trying on costumes that didn't fit, or were in the wrong colour, or which split during a performance (though of course, that could still happen) had plagued me for weeks.

By now you may have got the picture that I was pretty busy. So when Hollins had rolled up one morning and announced that he needed to go away for three weeks, I was none too chuffed.

Apparently his father had died and Hollins needed to go to his village for the funeral, so I could hardly complain.

It was incredibly inconvenient for me (and his father I suppose) as, at the time, I still had a load of stuff to do for the play and with Nancy arriving for her holiday within two weeks, I had been hoping to have everything ship-shape by then.

Anyway, Hollins arranged for his nephew to come and work for us during his absence. The nephew arrived, did one good days' work and was never seen again.

Ziggy then sent over one of the 'lads' from his site to come and at least clean the floors and do the washing. What an experience *that* was.

His name was Sixpence (?!?) The 60-something-year-old diminutive Zambian duly arrived in navy-blue overalls and steel-toe-capped boots to do the housework.

Now his language was something to behear – the audio version of behold, you know. It certainly wasn't difficult to understand his English. It was f'in' this and f'in' that, and "When the white people ran this f'in' country at least we had f'in' food on our plates." Needless to say, I kept the kids *well* away from Sixpence given their propensity for picking up on 'new' words. My mother would freak out if she heard what came out of Sixpence's mouth. I wasn't too happy listening to it myself for that matter. He may not have had a very clean mouth but at least he managed to clean the house so I didn't complain.

Thankfully I heard from our new gardener Jackman (Hollins' cousin) that Hollins would be back after two weeks, not three. Was I ever grateful for *that*.

Fortunately another area of omission was also rectified before the arrival of Nancy for her holiday.

One evening Ziggy returned home with a very smug look on his face and a large box in his arms. The no-longer-Christmas Crate had arrived!

We were astounded to find that nothing had been broken or stolen and it clearly had not been examined by Customs. (I think someone knew people in the right places.)

Apart from the anticipated contents it contained a very nice surprise in the way of an enormous block of Cheddar cheese. Given that it had been sitting in the crate, probably in some steaming warehouse, for weeks on end it was in remarkably good condition. Okay, it was a bit melted round the edges, but even that was no big deal, as I could use it for cheese sauce.

As we unpacked this crate, the kids thought it was Christmas all over again, but without the tree.

26

Dear All,

I have no idea where we are.

You may wonder why I'm writing, rather than typing this. It is because we are currently at 16,000ft somewhere over Zambia and I couldn't fit the typewriter in my hand baggage.

We are on our way to Mfuwe Lodge in the South Luangwa National Park to do a spot of game viewing.

Oh, you may have gathered by now that my mum arrived safe and sound. The little terrors were thrilled to see their Nanny – we had been winding them up about her visit for a week or so before she arrived. We didn't dare tell them earlier than that because having no concept of time they would have driven us nuts on an "are we there yet?" theme.

Anyway we had to get up at 4:30 this morning to get to the airport in time for our 7:00 flight south to Lusaka from where, after a three and a half hour wait, we continued our journey north-east in a 48-seater twin-prop job to Mfuwe Airport.

After landing and collecting our luggage everyone piled into a bus, and for about half an hour we travelled along a fairly well constructed dirt road to get to the park boundary and then the Lodge. When we arrived we were thrilled to be greeted by an enormous, real live elephant standing in the car park. Everyone wanted to leap out and take photographs, but the driver first warned us not to get close as, whilst it had chosen to place itself in the proximity of a group of buildings and people, it was still a wild elephant. And that if we got too close not only would it be wild, it would be bloody furious and probably charge us. (Not money, we already paid for our accommodation!)

Oh, sod this. I'm only going to tell you all about it when I get home and have access to my typewriter. This handwriting stuff is for the dogs. (Can dogs hold pens?)

Mfuwe Lodge consisted of several semidetached wooden chalets surrounding the main facility, which comprised reception/shop, a lounge/bar and dining room. The facilities were quite basic but pleasant.

A large area overlooked the Mfuwe Lagoon, which was home to some creatures and watering-hole to many more. Immediately in front of the lodge grounds the lagoon water butted against a dam-type façade, presumably to prevent the various animals from walking straight out of the water to enjoy the human company. Otherwise the lagoon was mostly surrounded by trees and bushes.

In the water we could see hippos, well their ears at least, as the rest of the head and body was completely submerged. I privately wondered if hippos could breathe through their ears. Every so often one would raise its head out of the water and yawn expansively, exposing massive tusks and a cavernous mouth large enough to swallow a small car. These visual displays were interspersed by a strange hippo communication which sounded like a very stout old-English gentleman slowly laughing "haw, haw, haw, haw, haw" at a modest witticism. There were also lots of birds, many heard but not seen and vice versa, which at future times we became quite interested in spotting and identifying.

And there were masses of monkeys. Some of them were almost as big as the kids and the males had bright blue balls. We had been warned not to encourage the monkeys as they were highly accomplished thieves and could inflict a nasty bite if challenged whilst conducting their thievery.

Our accommodation included all meals, but games drives were to be paid for as and when required. These were conducted in open top Land Rovers with three tiers of seats, the lower level containing the driver/game ranger (quite important) and two passengers, then two more benches for three people each, the highest level naturally being at the rear.

The lodge operated organised drives three times a day. Morning drives, when you had to get up with the birds for a cup of tea before departing at

5:30am and enjoying breakfast on arriving back, afternoon drives about an hour before dusk and having dinner on return, and night-drives which went out after dinner, when you might see animals that aren't normally out and about during the daytime.

Or you could simply stay at the lodge and watch the wildlife that came to drink at the lagoon.

It was a very interesting four days. For a start they weren't wrong about the monkeys.

On more than one occasion, when the kids were walking around with lollypops, a monkey would dash up and swipe it out of their hand. We had to impress upon them very quickly that if that should happen, they must not resist. As I'm sure you can imagine, the youngsters were not too impressed by this instruction. They soon changed to eating polo fruits instead.

One morning we were sitting at a table in the middle of the dining room eating breakfast when a monkey crept onto the ledge of an open window. Sitting there wearing a furrowed brow of concentration, it observed the current situation then in a flash leapt silently across two empty tables before landing on the back of Nancy's chair. In the blink of an eye it reached over her shoulder and stole a piece of toast off her plate, before high-tailing it, quite literally, back from whence it came.

I just sat there watching the whole scenario unfurl, mouth agape, just about to shout words of warning but it was all over before I could utter a word. It was the biggest wonder my mother didn't have a heart attack.

The expression of the lion being 'the king of the jungle' is rather a strange figure of speech, as the folk living there did not use the term 'jungle' but referred to it as 'the bush'.

I don't recall having any preconceived ideas of what the African bush would be like, but if I did have, they definitely wouldn't have been anywhere close to what we experienced.

On our first venture into the bush we had only been gone 20 minutes when the driver said we could be in for a severe storm and suggested we return to the lodge and ditch the roofless Land Rover for the 24-seater bus (even though there were only eight of us). As it turned out it didn't rain at all but because the bus couldn't negotiate some of the poorer roads, we hardly saw anything of interest, apart from scores of impala (a tan coloured antelope with a horizontal paler sand colour along its lower flank) and a herd of zebra.

By the time we returned to the lodge it was dark. After a drink at the bar Nancy and I chose to go and get changed for dinner, leaving Ziggy to look after the kids. Leon thought otherwise and kept calling, "I want to come with you."

The chalets were about 100 yards or so from the main buildings.

As we walked I was telling Nancy about a chat I had just had with another guest. He and his friends had driven to Mfuwe so had been doing their game viewing in their own car. Just as they were returning to the lodge they hit the jackpot and came across a family of lions; male lion, lioness and three or four cubs. He said they were not far from the lodge.

As a regular visitor, he also said that it wasn't unusual to find the spoor (paw-print tracks) of lion having wandered through the lodge grounds at night.

It was only then that I had discovered there was no form of protective fencing around Mfuwe Lodge.

Given our location at the time I was relating this to her, Nancy was a bit perturbed by this information. However, as the pathways were well lit and the chalets had outside lights, I wasn't too worried. I mean, surely the management wouldn't allow people to just wander around willy-nilly on their own if there was any likelihood of bumping into a lion or two along the way?

We had almost reached our chalets when, totally without warning, there was the most horrific crack of lightning and all the lights went out.

Trying not to panic, we stumbled on in the direction of our rooms when I heard Leon screaming somewhere behind us. I thought he had gone back to his Dad.

I immediately turned back to try to find him, telling him to keep very still and just shout at me so that I could track him down. I was terrified that if he wandered off in the wrong direction he could finish up in the lagoon with the hippos and God only knows what else with nasty pointy teeth. I actually hadn't needed to tell him to shout as he was screaming "Mummy! Mummy! Mummy!" at the top of his voice.

But the plan worked and I picked him up and headed for Nancy's chalet.

We set about getting changed since that is what we had gone to do in the first place. Leaving Leon with Nancy, I nipped next door to my room. Well, 'nipped' is a bit off the mark.

First we had to track down the candles, of which there were two in each room for such emergencies. I had barely left the porch when the candle blew out so had to go back for a re-light. I tried again, taking Nancy's lighter with me as insurance.

I quickly reached my room and got changed. Just as I was about to leave, the heavens opened and it *sheeted* down.

Luckily the wall dividing the two chalets was so thin one could easily conduct a conversation between the rooms. I asked Nancy to stand under the cover of her porch, as close to the edge as possible, holding her remaining candle as a beacon, to enable me to find my way back in the dark, since I would be unable to keep my candle alight in the pouring rain.

With a large towel draped over my head and shoulders I made it back just before the wind snuffed her candle out yet again, but now we were stuck. All I could think about was the possibility of these bloody lions strolling through the grounds in the pitch dark. And although it wasn't that far to the main buildings, we figured it was far enough for us to get gobbled up by a hungry lion.

So we decided to sit tight until the lights came back on, or someone rescued us with umbrellas and torches. Fat chance.

After being stuck in the chalet FOR AN HOUR AND A HALF with neither food nor drink, we were all for standing out on the porch and shouting for help, when the power was restored.

With towels suitably draped over us (it was still hosing down) we raced back to the main building to find Ziggy, Brad and Vicki quietly finishing off their dinner.

Were we ever cheesed off!

Ziggy couldn't understand why we were so worried about being eaten by lions, since we had obviously returned quite safely.

However, once we had finished our dinner Ziggy felt obliged to be the one to put the kids to bed. Nancy and I stayed at the bar to catch up on some drinks. But this just wasn't meant to be our night.

The severity of the storm had driven all the Mfuwe insects into the bar. And the mosquitoes were holding a convention at our table. As fast as we sat swatting mozzies off our legs, they were attacking our arms. We finished up with so many red blotches you'd think we had measles.

When we eventually returned to our chalets we were horrified to see *millions* of insects swarming around the doors. Hardly surprising when you consider the attraction of the outside lights positioned above the door frame. We had great difficulty in keeping the blighters out of the chalets when we entered, despite the fly screen doors.

Luckily the beds were equipped with mosquito nets, but to get inside them without the mozzies joining you was a work of art in itself. Still, it all added to the excitement of life in the wild.

After a cup of tea at the crack of dawn the next day, Nancy, the kids and I piled into the Land Rover and went off in search of interesting things. After about half an hour, we found an interesting thing. And what a BIG one it was.

The driver took us down a spur (a short dirt road) which culminated in a circle, rather like a traffic roundabout but without any traffic or pretty flowers in the centre. When he parked up we were about three or four metres above the ground below. No, that sounds bad. We weren't up a tree or anything, but the ground at the edge of the spur sloped quite seriously downwards.

Being proficient in this game-spotting lark, the driver soon spied a rhino. When we saw it, it was difficult to understand how we could have missed it. It was a GIGANTIC male. Almost as big as the vehicle in which we sat.

Then the driver began to traverse the incredibly steep slope to get a closer look. Personally I was happy to have stayed where we were and stick to binoculars for a close-up. The rhinoseroseroserus, as our bunch called it, was on the other side of a row of bushes and as we drove nearer to it the driver whispered that we must keep absolutely quiet, as whilst a rhino's eyesight wasn't up to much, its hearing and sense of smell were acute and he didn't want it searching us out. HE didn't?

The five of us had commandeered the back tier of the Land Rover; there were another three people on the second level and a 'foreign' old bloke

(Bulgarian, I think) sitting at the lowest level next to the driver.

We all sat quietly (even the kids) watching the rhino slowly chomping his way through the grass and he eventually ambled past the bushes until he was at a position between us and the spur, effectively cutting off our escape route which, quite frankly, I found a bit disconcerting.

It was at this point that the foreign prat on the front seat produced a packet full of lollypops which he generously and vociferously offered to everyone in the vehicle. As much as we tried to hush him up, he was twisting around in his seat and rustling the packet inviting all on board, especially the kids, to help themselves.

Everyone eventually took one just to keep the old fart quiet. Next there was a crackling of plastic wrappers followed by the bloke shaking his packet again for the rubbish to be placed in it, which he then noisily scrunched up.

I had no doubt that if we were detected and the rhino decided to ram the Land Rover, it would have had no trouble whatsoever in turning the whole thing on its side complete with occupants. If I could have reached him I would have clouted this old bugger, but I personally didn't want to make any sudden movements, poor eyesight or no poor eyesight.

As the rhino eventually moved on, the ranger engaged his 4-wheel-drive and got us back up the embankment. We drove on for another hour or so during which time we saw several confusions (I kid you not) of guinea fowl with bright blue faces, a small herd of zebra, stacks of baboons and two elephants at a distance.

The most entertainment came from a couple of families, or 'sounders', of warthogs. Grumpy-looking daddy warthogs with mean curved tusks and long faces followed by mummy warthogs which in turn were followed by several baby warthogs. They were all covered in dark grey/brown rough hair and had a mane like a horse except that it stretched from their ears along their necks and back, almost to their tails. The daddy warthogs' manes were really long.

As they ran, the warthogs' tails stuck up in the air like poles, with little tufts on the end resembling tattered flags. The children were absolutely entranced and delighted by these miniature four-legged flag carriers, as they ran off at great speed into the bush.

With all that and the rhino experience we felt we'd had more than enough entertainment for one day and spent the afternoon at the swimming pool, though even that area wasn't devoid of potential hazards.

As the kids played nearby, having great fun kicking up the ankle-deep dried leaves on the ground, a member of staff hastily warned against such a practice, saying that there were likely to be scorpions lurking unseen in there, not to mention the possibility of well-camouflaged snakes.

Then a guide mentioned that only the week before they had found signs that a hippo had been in the swimming pool, though hastened to add that this would have been during the night as they do not leave the lagoon until after dark to go foraging for food.

On the last day of our stay at Mfuwe Lodge, we took the dawn drive again. We initially didn't see anything too unusual, just more impala than you could shake a stick at, and other buck type stuff as well as some more warthogs. Talking of which, we'd had roast warthog on the menu the night before and it was very tasty, although I would have thought it was illegal to eat it, this being a National Reserve and all.

A few kilometres out of camp we chanced upon a lion and lioness on the side of the road, which the game ranger informed us were in the mating phase. We shortly established this, and after witnessing the intriguing ritual for ten minutes, moved further along.

Thirty minutes and six elephants later we turned round and headed for the Lodge to have breakfast and then prepare for our departure.

A few kilometres later we reached the spot where the lions were, except this time they were in the middle of the road.

The driver put on his brakes and waited for them to move. Hah.

After several minutes he revved his engine to try to encourage them to shift. Double Hah! Knowing that time was now getting a little tight he began thumping on his door (apparently hooting was not a good idea).

Taking the hint, the lioness reluctantly moved off to the right side of the road. With a very pissed off look on his face, the lion eventually strolled slightly to the left. I was 'fortunate enough' to be sitting in prime position on the left side of the raised back seat.

The driver slowly eased forward but I think the lion was a bit more agitated about having his sex life disturbed than was initially perceived by the driver, because as we drew closer the lion opened his cavernous, carnivorous mouth and with his lips curled back, exposed the biggest set of gnashers I have ever clapped eyes on.

If that wasn't enough to scare the living daylights out of everyone, especially me being the closest, he then started to go down on his haunches, as if getting ready to spring.

At that point the driver floored the accelerator THANK GOD and we roared off (if you'll pardon the pun) down the road. I swear to you, the lion was SO close to me as we passed it I could smell its rank breath.

As we arrived at the lodge I was still in quite a state of shock and my legs were shaking so much I could barely climb off the Land Rover, never mind walk to the dining room. It was as well this happened on the last morning of our little holiday because I don't think I'd have had the courage to go out again after that experience. Oh, the joys of the wild in Africa.

On a comparative note, watching the swans glide sedately down the River Trent by the Pleasure Gardens in my home town will never seem quite so captivating again.

27

April 1981
Dear Lots of People,
*   You may have noticed a marked lack in communications*
of late. Various events and wonderful times spent with UK
visitors have curtailed my letter writing.
*   After returning from our exciting game viewing trip,*
the next big thing to hit our agenda on the twenty third
of March was the grand occasion of Vicki and Leon turning
three years old. It seems like they have been around a
lot longer to me, and I mean that in the nicest possible
way.

Due to a lack of party hats and other accoutrements in Kitwe shops, we needed to be quite inventive to make this birthday something special. Nancy and I decided to give the party a Mr Men theme.

Invitations were handed out to about a dozen or more children, many of whom would be accompanied by a mother. Our next task was to set about making party hats. Each 'hat' consisted of a decorated band of cardboard with a square attached at the front displaying one of the Mr Men characters. We had our work seriously cut out making and putting them all together, especially as we could only do this whilst the children were at school or in bed.

And we had to make the birthday cake. With imagination now totally deplete, we made it in the shape of a large number 3. And as per all kids' preferences it was a chocolate cake, suitably decorated. We hid it in my wardrobe until the due day and just hoped it would not melt all over my clothes in the meantime.

As the little guests arrived on Monday afternoon each chose a Mr Men hat to wear. Our lot had already chosen theirs. Vicki chose Mr Bump and Leon appropriately enough chose Mr Chatterbox. Brad, being the BIG brother, opted for Mr Strong. Then we had Misters Nosy, Tickle, Silly, Grumpy, Tall, Bounce, Sneeze, Lazy, Greedy, Messy, Muddle and the infamous-at-Heathrow-Airport Mr Small.

The hats were held in place by sticky tape. NO, we didn't tape them to the kids' heads, we sticky-taped the ends of the bands together to the appropriate size to fit each child's head.

As usual a large variety of games, some musical, some otherwise, were played and thoroughly enjoyed by the kids, leaving the supervising grown-ups totally knackered. I'm not sure what time everyone left, but so long as they did that was good enough for me.

We then had time for a few days of winding down before Nancy returned to what we knew would be a warm welcome and lots of questions at the pub. For our part we would miss her happy, smiling face in our midst.

No sooner had my mum departed than we had to start planning for the arrival of Doris, my grandmother. Having always been her favourite, Leon could hardly contain his excitement at the prospect of Nannan's visit.

For some reason best known to Zambia Airways the evening leg of her flight from Lusaka to the Copperbelt was flying into Ndola Airport as opposed to Kitwe. The open stretch of the 55km distance between Kitwe and Ndola had quite a reputation for hold-ups, and I do not mean delays, during the hours of darkness, so Ziggy suggested that it would be better if I did not go with him to the airport.

Leaving Hollins to babysit the children, Ziggy dropped me off at the theatre on his way out saying he would bring Doris there before we went home.

I was fine with that as there was bound to be someone I knew who I could chat to for the couple of hours the collection would take.

I don't think I have mentioned this before, but apparently the theatre club was renowned, according to non-members, for marriage break-ups. Armed with this information Ziggy and I were very careful not to mix with what could be 'the wrong company'. It had been mooted by Molly that those involved in the actual acting side of the Theatre Club were more prone than most to wander in this direction, having gained extra confidence and in some cases fame, on stage. Ziggy and I vowed to stick to working back-stage.

When I arrived at the Club that night there were only two customers whom I knew. One was Brian the Club 'dandy'. You know the type, cravat and blazer, slicked back hair. Another was a guy called Andy who also worked for Rhinestone and who arrived with his wife and one-year old kid not long after us. He had immediately taken to the acting stuff and in fact was the leading male in the current production.

Sitting talking to him was a very punk brassy bint who was out from the UK visiting her sister. Andy had obviously come to the Club straight from work because he was still in his work shorts.

As I sat chatting to Brian I noticed over his shoulder that the punk, who was sitting particularly close to Andy, was playing an 'imaginary tune' with her fingers – on his thigh. But the look on their faces and normal tone of conversation said butter wouldn't melt in their mouths.

As fascinated as I was by this performance, I convinced myself that I was reading more into it than was there and continued my conversation with Brian. I have always taken a dim view of gossip-mongering and believe in the principal of innocent until proven guilty.

After a short while the bint got off her bar stool and whispered something in Andy's ear, resulting in him answering, "Yes" in quite a normal tone. Then they both disappeared outside.

At one point I had caught a bit of their conversation where she was talking about trouble she was having with her car. I assumed they were going outside to have a look at it. I ask you, how naive can one get?

After about fifteen minutes Brian said to me, "Where do you think those two have got to then?"

"I was just wondering that myself," I replied, "but didn't want to mention it."

"If they're not back in five minutes," said Brian, "I'm going out to look for them."

True to his word, five minutes later Brian upped and wandered off outside. He was soon back, chuckling away to himself, and promptly announced that the two of them were having it off under the swing in the kids' playground.

Now Brian *could* be a bit of a scandalmonger, so I said that I didn't believe him.

"It's true. You go outside and look around the corner and you can see them. Well, actually all you can see are four feet and a bare arse."

"Oh, yes," says I, "and what if, as I am peeping around the corner, they are on their way back in? What do I say, that, 'I was just out for a breath of fresh air', or that, 'I wanted to make it a threesome'?"

Needless to say, I didn't bother to check on his story.

Shortly afterwards Glyn arrived, whereupon Brian immediately told him the story and suggested he go and check. Glyn graciously declined.

Next in was Mike, and Brian was almost falling over himself to pass on the story and to get someone – anyone – to go and check it out. Mike quite took to the story, but was still a little reluctant.

I now need to describe to you the physical layout of the Theatre Club bar. The long rear wall of the bar-room had a ventilation gap in the wall, about a foot deep just below ceiling height, which ran the entire length of the wall. Being unglazed – to allow the fresh air in – it was criss-crossed with metal bars, like XXXX, to keep the burglars out. It just so happened that the kiddies' playground was directly on the other side of this wall.

In a bid to get somebody to verify his story, Brian suggested to Mike that he looked through the crisscross bars to observe the 'goings on' and testify that he wasn't telling pork pies (Cockney rhyming slang for 'lies').

Mike duly climbed onto a nearby table and tried to look through the bars. Unfortunately he is a bit on the short side and couldn't get high enough to see.

Not to be thwarted, Brian then indicated the log pile stacked against the wall and which had been increasing in height in readiness for a fire in the coming winter, and which was higher than the table.

Pointing to it, Brian said, "Just stand on that lot."

Mike gingerly ascended the stack of wood then, teetering on the top, duly looked through the 'spy window'.

Almost bursting at the seams and in danger of scattering the entire log pile across the room, he climbed down.

"It's true!" he stage-whispered. "They're really at it!"

124

Several other members came into the Club during the next ten minutes and of course were all told the story. Most of them then also climbed onto the log pile to enjoy the show.

This was turning into a marathon session, and if nothing else I had to be impressed by the stamina of the fornicating duo in the appropriately named playground.

By now the entire room was rocking with people trying not to give the game away by laughing out too loud, since the noise in the bar would easily have carried through this unglazed spy hole, assuming that Andy and the punk were in any frame of mind to hear anything apart from gasps, moans and heavy breathing.

After about another five minutes, the energetic couple nonchalantly returned to take up their previous seats at the bar. Admitted they did come in a minute or so apart, but she was looking rather dishevelled, and he was a tad 'flushed'.

It was all the rest of us could do to keep from erupting. My stomach ached abominably with suppressed laughter.

They sat and had a drink together and then sod me if they didn't disappear outside once again! I really don't know how we controlled ourselves, but we all agreed that, in true theatre style, they must have just come in for a refreshment break.

By the time Ziggy and Doris arrived, the copulating couple had left, but the place was still in an uproar. The bar was about to close, but stayed open for at least another half hour in Doris's honour, whilst the story of Andy, the Punk and the Woodpile was related to them.

What a start to Doris's holiday! She announced that just listening to the tale was the most fun she'd had in years, and she could see she was in for a wonderful time.

A few days before the end of Doris's visit the latest issue of *Prompt Copy* was released.

Prompt Copy was the Club magazine published each month. It contained news regarding current or past productions, the odd article of theatrical interest together with other bits and pieces, and a regular section headed 'Overheard at the Bar' where quips were contributed (usually anonymously) by Club members and which I'm sure needs no explanation.

Recent 'Overheards':

Moderately well-known Producer to well-known Props girl, "It's not big enough. I must have a bigger one!"

And,

(male) Housekeeper talking to rather large lady Bar Manager with some dubious habits, "Tables are meant for glasses, Madam, not arses!"

This month there was a slight variation on the theme. Instead of *Overheard at the Bar* it became *Overlooked from the Bar*.

"There are those amongst us who put their new found youthful vigour and fame to remarkable use. The view from the log pile is rather entertaining – or so I am told." Anon

Naturally all those 'in the know' fell about when they read this. We couldn't wait to see Andy's reaction when he read it. I was lucky enough to be there when someone offered him a copy of the mag, asking if he'd had chance to read it yet.

"Yes," he said.

Brian asked, "Have you read all of the articles?"

"Yes!"

"Well, did you see this one?" persisted Brian, actually pointing out the relevant lines in the mag.

"Yes," insisted Andy, with a mystified look.

By this time everyone in the bar was exploding with laughter. Andy obviously had no idea that everyone at the Club was aware of his antics.

Brian took him by the shoulder, turned him to face the woodpile and said, "Well, just imagine what you might see one night if you stood upon there and looked through the gap!"

Tick … tick … tick.

Andy's face was a picture, a puce-coloured picture actually, of comprehension and then anger, as he realised that everyone had been and still was, laughing at him. I thought for a moment that he was going to seriously stick one on Brian, but thankfully he grinned and turning to his captive audience, simply said, "You rotten buggers" as we all howled with laughter.

We never let him forget about it. Fortunately his wife never got to hear about it, but I reckoned anyone thinking of any shenanigans at the Theatre Club in the future might have had a few second thoughts.

28

April 1981

Dear Nancy and Mev,

Having managed an hour's snooze this afternoon I figured it was time that I dropped you a short note.

The Queen Mother is now well and truly In Residence and has quickly settled into her holiday accommodation. She is especially pleased to be reunited with her little Spiderbum and Leon is equally thrilled to be with his beloved Nannan.

As was to be expected, it hasn't taken long for our 79-year-old to be enthralling everyone at the Club, where her similarity in age and build to the QM has not gone unnoticed. She is currently reclining on the settee reading, most unQM-like, one of her Mills and Boons. Although we fear to bring the subject up, I think she is missing the television.

So far we haven't done anything particularly special. I am sure it goes without saying that we've been to the Club most days or nights, or both, but not much besides. She naturally comes with me when I go shopping, but usually stays in the car with the kids and amuses herself observing the local colour. Contrary to her preconceptions she is now of the opinion that the majority of the local people dress very smartly and is quite taken up with the civility of the place, which I find quite amazing as some thieving bastard nicked her knitting bag two days after her arrival.

The bag in question contained a three-quarters finished matinee coat I had asked her to knit for Margaret's baby, all her knitting needles, patterns, etc, also her mirror, baby lotion, gold watch and the kitchen sink.

We couldn't remember if it was left on a table in the copper bar of the Club, or maybe it fell out of the car in the car park, but when we returned to the Club to look for it three hours later there was no sign of it – which didn't surprise anyone!

It was a couple of weeks before we were able to get replacement needles and wool so all she had been able to do was read, and I think she got Mills and Boon-ed out.

Still, she can't be all that put off by this quiet life, as she's already talking about coming out for Christmas. If she does, we'll have no problem getting her ticket from this end, which brings me onto the next subject.

George Ndube was a friend of ours who was the 30-year-old manager at Zambia Airways Kitwe office.

I'd been talking to George before Doris's arrival to make sure somebody met her at Lusaka airport before flying on to Ndola, which he kindly agreed to do, even though we'd bought her ticket via an independent travel agent. He was in the Club when we took Doris there the day after she arrived and always chatted with her whenever we met up.

After Doris had been with us for about a week, George told Ziggy one night that he was so enchanted with her that he wanted to take her out for dinner. Ziggy told me, but we didn't mention it to Doris, as we both agreed that George would probably change his mind once his couple of whiskies had worn off.

A few days later we were all at the Club when George, sitting at the bar, called me over and asked when he could take Doris out. We set the date for the following Tuesday night, when I would bring Doris to the Club and he would take her out from there.

George was talking to her later, and when he told her what we had arranged she didn't take him seriously. However, when I spoke to her later, and confirmed that it was organised, she didn't know what to make of it.

"I haven't been asked out on a date in 60 years," she said, with a silly grin on her face "but I'm not sure about this, I hardly know him!"

Eventually I persuaded her it was all above board and that George was a perfectly respectable, nice chap, so she agreed to go.

After that, every time we saw George he would say,

"Don't forget about Tuesday."

During the course of a later conversation with George when I mentioned that it was a pity Doris wasn't staying longer in Zambia, he said he would try to get her ticket extended if he could, at the same time asking me if I would like to join them for the Tuesday Dinner. Not being one to turn down a free nosh I naturally agreed. Doris was visibly relieved.

George offered us a choice of three dining establishments. I opted for one I had not been to before.

Regrettably it was a BIG mistake. George ordered a T-bone steak which he could barely eat, whilst Doris and I opted for fillet, which also left a lot to be desired. I didn't think anyone could stuff up a fillet steak, but …

Despite the food we had a lovely night out, with George entertaining us with many tales of strange travels and travellers, and Doris was delighted with her 'date'. I felt a bit bad when George came to pay the bill for the lousy food, but figured that with the potential of all our future travels he would probably be able to put it down to Zambia Airways' account as a good investment.

One thing which surprised me was my grandmother's eating habits. One evening she walked into the lounge, after passing by the kitchen where Ziggy was making a curry.

"My word," she said, "that smells nice."

I never would have expected her to like curry. In fact while she was with us she ate so many things she had never tried before, that I was in total awe. At 79 she had taken on, for the first time in her life – curry, biltong, samosas, green peppers, spaghetti bolognaise, garlic bread, the list was endless. And she enjoyed them all!

One evening Doris was putting the kids to bed and Ziggy was cooking. Brad lay on the settee moaning about his poorly foot. Nobody could figure out what was wrong with it, but he'd moaned about it the day before too. However, we were not too worried as we couldn't see anything obvious and in between times he had been tearing about all over the garden, showing no signs of pain. We thought he might just be looking for a bit of fuss.

The school broke up for the Easter holidays on the 10th April for four weeks and I did some odd sessions of reading with Brad during that time and noticed that his hearing was not as good as it should have been. He'd had an ear infection a while before, so I took him back to the doctor who checked him out. She said his right ear seemed back to normal, but he was slightly deaf in his left ear and that it might warrant an operation, though it could probably wait until our contract was up in August 1982.

However, as it might be getting worse, she suggested I got a second opinion.

This diagnosis was confirmed, suggesting it might be a condition known as 'glue ear' which apparently was quite common in kids of Brad's age. The second doc said he would probably need to see an ENT specialist to have grommets inserted.

As there were no such facilities for that in Zambia, we figured it might warrant an appointment with a specialist in South Africa or even England. The latter was obviously our preferred option, but first we had to find out if Rhinestone would pay for the flights. Tickets from Zambia to England were not cheap.

Just prior to Doris's arrival I had a personal sewing splurge. I made a pair of shorts for Ziggy, two pairs each for Brad and Leon, two skirts for Vicki, three dresses for myself and a shirt for one of Brad's friends (birthday present).

I also needed to make myself a special dress in preparation for the NKAS Awards Ball in the not too distant future. After Doris's arrival I was not sure that I liked the dress I had made, so I determined to make another one.

Before I could do that however, I had a mammoth task to perform because Doris wanted me to make her a couple of dresses, too.

This had proved to be a daunting task in the past for reasons chiefly involving her shape, but when you consider that in Zambia I had no dress patterns in her size, with not a snowball's chance in hell of buying any, it was even worse than previous. My only course of action was to try and make up a pattern from one of her existing dresses.

Unfortunately I had no-one to blame but myself for this situation, having mentioned that I had seen some rather nice fabric which she would like.

I was running short of meat again and as we needed to go to Chingola for the dress material, I figured I might as well get the meat there too. But this time I would be better prepared so on Wednesday I phoned the butchers to place an order for Thursday. Smart move, eh?

When I phoned I was quite surprised to get straight through. Well, straight through to the butcher, but it took me three attempts before I finally got connected to the person who took the orders for meat.

Our conversation went like this:

"I'd like to place an order for some meat, to collect tomorrow."

"Yes, Madam, where are you phoning from?"

"Kitwe."

"Yes, Madam, what company?"

"No company, it is just for me."

"Just for you? Very good Madam, what would you like?"

"Five kilograms of fillet steak."

"Three kilos of rump steak."

"No, five kilos of fillet steak."

"How many?"

"Five."

"I'm sorry, I can't hear you. How many?"

Background noise, crashing of trays and people shouting.

"FIVE."

"I'm sorry?"

"One, two, three, four, FIVE."

"I see. Five kilos of rump steak."

"No. Five kilos of FILLET steak."

"Ah. Five kilos of fillet steak."

Drained. "Yes."

"That's a lot of meat for one person. You must have a large appetite Madam, (ha ha ha)."

Just what I need, a witty butcher.

"It is for my entire family, not just for me alone."

"Oh, I see. Sorry, Madam. Anything else for the Madam?"

More background noises sounding like 60 maniacs let loose with cleavers.

"Yes, a three kilo joint of rump."

"Three?"

"Yes."

"Three kilos of rump steak."

"Three kilos of rump in a JOINT."

"I didn't hear you."

"I want the rump in one large piece."

"Six kilos of ... I'm sorry, Madam, the line is terrible, I can't hear what you are saying. Can you just come in the morning after eight hours and we'll be able to sell you some meat."

"Will you have plenty of meat?"

"I can't hear you."

"DO YOU EXPECT TO HAVE A LOT OF MEAT?"

"The line is terrible."

"Okay, I'll come in tomorrow."

"I can't hear you. Can you come in tomorrow?"

I collapsed over the dining table in the sheer exasperation of this frustrating conversation and decided to 'go in tomorrow' regardless.

We managed to get the meat and enough material for *three* dresses for Doris! Lucky me!

May 1981
Dear Nancy & Mev and anyone else around,
Doris and I have just got back from a trip to the Zambia Airways office in town. Much to her disappointment Doris's toy-boy (George) was unable to change the date of her return flight.

After my last letter to you, Brad had continued to complain about his feet hurting, but we could still see nothing amiss. However on Friday he was getting around by shuffling about on his bum. At bath time I noticed a rash around his ankles and by Saturday afternoon this had spread virtually all the way up his legs. Time to call in the doc.

Her diagnosis, confirmed by a doctor at the mine-owned Chibaluma Hospital, was rheumatic fever. He was admitted on the spot although the diagnosis would only be confirmed when they could carry out a series of tests on Monday. I wanted to stay there with him, but wasn't allowed. Brad was quite upset, as was I for that matter.

The upshot of it all is that they put him on antibiotics and kept him in for the week to make sure it was cleared up without any complications setting in. Apparently rheumatic fever is linked to streptococcus throat, though what the throat has to do with leg rashes and aching joints I do not know.

By Friday the spots were all but gone and he'd not had any pain in his ankles since they started the antibiotics, so he was allowed home.

They all went back to school today and the instant Brad got inside he ran up to his teacher, proud as punch and announced, "I've been in the hospital all by myself and I've been in for SIX days."

My grandmother's visit took quite a different format from that of my Mum, as we didn't really do anything 'special' with her. Any notion to go game viewing was quickly discounted given her portly frame and elderly legs. The mental picture of Doris clambering in and out of a Land Rover was enough to put the keenest nature-lover off going to the game park.

Fortunately she was easily entertained. She happily spent most of her time watching the antics of her three great-grandchildren and when she wasn't doing that she was knitting. When one of the Club members heard that her knitting bag had gone missing she kindly found some spare needles and patterns which she gave to Doris and then pointed us in the direction of a shop selling wool. One happy camper.

There was one event which she was delighted to be able to attend, the Nkana Kitwe Art Society Awards Ball, an important annual affair. Members of the Awards Committee attended each production throughout the year and at the end of the year they got together to discuss who deserved the awards for best actor / actress, supporting actor / actress, newcomer, producer, stage manager, over-all production, etc. Out of a total of 12 awards, The Crucible took seven of them, including Best Production and Best Costumes – which I was thrilled about. To quote:

"The Committee would like to thank Gill Lonsdale for all her help in the wardrobe over the past twelve months, but it was the unanimous decision of the Committee that the Award for Best Costumes be given to Ann Patras for her costumes in The Crucible."

I can tell you I felt about ten feet tall, and twice as embarrassed when I walked up to receive the engraved Copper Plate Trophy.

I wrote a short letter to Nancy a couple of days later, telling her about it.

The Awards event included a hot buffet and culminated in drinking and dancing and there was a band playing who were very good. They must have been because even Ziggy said so and as you know he is not overly forthcoming with his compliments, but he was up and dancing within the first ten minutes. We all had oceans to drink and eventually left the party still in full swing at 2:00am.

Ziggy had to get up at 5:00 on Sunday morning to take one of his boys to the airport. I didn't wake until eight, and as the kids were all racing about, I must have been out solid. At some point I got up, took two paracetamols and went back to bed.

After calling in on the site, Ziggy got home at 9:15 and set about making us all a full-on fried breakfast. Normally that would be guaranteed to cure any hangover, but this time I was a lost cause.

Once everyone had eaten Ziggy collapsed on the bed and five minutes later I did the same on Vicki's bed. Of Doris there was not a sound. The children were again left to their own devices.

I eventually resurfaced at about half past eleven and was amazed and relieved to see that no damage had befallen anyone or anything. Doris remained out of it until 2pm. When she did get up she swore blind she was suffering from gin poisoning. This was one of those days where any resemblance to the real Queen Mother went completely out the window.

Oh, I've just read what I wrote above, and should explain that everyone had not eaten Ziggy — just the food he made.

I think I'd better stop this letter right now. It's not making much sense.

Doris's holiday drew to a close and was rounded off with a last minute shopping rush to buy some 'special things' to take home, such as a pineapple and 'something copper'. On the morning of her departure she also had me scaling the lemon and *naartjie* trees for supplies of fruit.

She left as she arrived, via the Theatre Club bar. A large crowd of her newly acquired friends had gathered to trade tearful kisses and goodbyes, with a firm promise from Doris to return the following year "but for longer next time," before she climbed reluctantly into Ziggy's car for the journey to the airport.

No-one would forget Doris in a hurry.

30

Dear All,

    Cokey seems to be earning his keep at last. Last Saturday our regular night guard didn't turn up. We were having a quiet night in and I heard Coke barking. I assumed he was barking at Brandy but then I heard her barking too, which is highly unusual.

    I got Ziggy to go and find out why they were barking so madly.

    It appeared that Rhinestone had organised a relief guard. But when he banged on the gate and couldn't get any response from us (we were listening to music) he entered the property by climbing over the wall.

    When Ziggy found him he was standing stock still, backed up to the kaya wall, whilst the two dogs barked and growled at him. What good dogs we have!

We were supposed to go to a fireworks display at the Convent the previous November, but it was cancelled due to the curfew. It was eventually rescheduled for the end of May so along we went.

Brad had always been terrified of fireworks, so after much ado, we found ourselves a spot to sit quite far away from the action. Much to our surprise – and delight – the display was excellent.

When we arrived home we found that yet again we had no night guard. After we'd driven inside and Ziggy went back to close and lock the gate, the guard appeared from behind a bush across the road. He obviously had no intention of climbing over the wall again. Whilst I was in some ways pleased that he was scared of our dogs it did beg the question: if the guard was scared of our two soppy dogs, exactly what use would he be in the event that we had burglars? After all, Brandy and Coke could hardly be classified as ferocious guard dogs like Dobermans or Rottweilers, they were just extra-hairy pets.

Ziggy went to bed at about 11. As I was recovering from a tonsil infection and was on antibiotics, I had taken a nap that afternoon so now wasn't at all tired. I stayed up to read my book until about 12:30.

I was almost ready to hop into bed when it occurred to me that I had forgotten to take my antibiotics, so went through to the kitchen to fetch a glass of water and the tablets.

When I opened the fridge door I heard Cokey get up from his bed outside the kitchen door and start barking. I thought he was barking at the new guard as a 'warning' that he shouldn't come near the house whilst I was up and about. But I decided that was crediting Cokey with amazing powers of deduction for any dog, never mind one so young.

Intrigued by the young dog's actions, I peeked through the scullery window beside the back door, to see where the guard was. I couldn't see him, but I could see Cokey on his hind legs, with his front paws up on the *naartjie* tree trunk, barking into the branches.

'Odd,' I thought.

The next minute *naartjies* began hurtling down from the tree. The bloody guard was up the tree, helping himself to our fruit! Now I don't mind sharing our garden produce when we obviously have far more than we can consume, but all he had to do was ask for some. Not help himself on the sly. That went against the principles I was brought up with. It was stealing.

And he clearly was not just taking enough to satisfy his appetite, he had enough to open a soddin' market stall!

The fact that someone who was supposed to be guarding us and our property was actually stealing it seemed counterproductive to the objective.

He eventually descended from the tree and collected his booty which was scattered on the driveway and stashed it by the *kaya*. Then he turned and headed towards the house.

I quickly moved away from the kitchen window and flattened myself against the wall between the utility sink and the door so he couldn't see me, being scantily clad in my underwear.

Then he came right up to the door and tried the handle. I knew I had locked it in preparation for going to bed but nevertheless I nearly sh*t myself.

When I heard him move away I very cautiously peered through the window over the sink and could see him messing about with the beer crates nearby.

There were two containing full beers and several crates of empties and he was shifting the bottles around.

I decided now was the time to alert Ziggy.

He reluctantly left his bed and came to look through the window saying he couldn't see anything wrong. Then he took himself off to the loo.

With the bathroom light switched on and the flushing of the toilet, the guard naturally beat a hasty retreat from the area. So when Ziggy looked into the yard from the far end of the house, where he could get a better view of the situation, there was nothing to see. He returned to bed.

I didn't. I stayed by the window.

Eventually the guard reappeared – right by the window. I nearly sh*t myself again. But he moved on and went back to rearranging bottles. I still hadn't figured out what he was trying to achieve by this weird behaviour.

After a lot of to-ing and fro-ing, he eventually helped himself to a bottle of Coke and stood there sipping it. So I dashed back to the bedroom and urged Ziggy to come and sort him out. FAT CHANCE.

I returned yet again to the kitchen and just as I was skirting the waste bin I saw his face pressed up against the window by the back door (where I had previously been standing!) and nearly sh*t myself for the *third* time.

136

I carefully looked around the corner only to see him try the door handle again and this time he pushed hard against the door. Then he bent down and looked through the keyhole and tried again to push the door open.

The bugger was seriously attempting to get in the house.

I had had enough. It was time to act. However I wasn't too keen to tackle him by myself as I didn't know how he would react. Like, he might attack me in a panic.

Ziggy HAD to do something now.

I went back again to the bedroom and after telling him what was going on Ziggy finally agreed to come. He donned a pair of shorts whilst I grabbed my dressing-gown and by the time we returned to the kitchen the guard had disappeared again.

Ziggy went outside and called for him. There was a long delay before he emerged from the back of the *kaya*. I suspected he had been looking for something with which to prize open the door.

When the guard eventually deigned to appear, Ziggy asked him what he had been doing by the back door.

"I don't know, sir."

Now what sort of an answer was that?

Next Ziggy asked him about taking the *naartjies*. He, of course, denied it. I could not stand there and listen to such drivel.

"Let us get one thing perfectly clear here," I said. "I was in the kitchen and I saw you through the window. You were helping yourself to *naartjies*."

"No, Madam."

"What do you mean 'no Madam'? I saw you, man. You were up the tree, this one here," I pointed, "and you were picking *naartjies* and throwing them to the ground. Then you climbed down from the tree, picked them all up and took them somewhere over there." I pointed again, in the general direction of the *kaya*.

"It wasn't me, Madam."

"Then who was it? Have you got a friend here with you? Or your brother, or your cousin?" I asked.

He laughed. "Ah, no Madam."

"Then it must have been you that I saw."

"No, Madam, it wasn't me."

"Next I saw you come over here, to these crates. You were messing about with the beer bottles then you took a bottle of coke and drank it."

"No, Madam, I was standing by the gate, guarding."

By now I was getting so angry I was shaking. My hands were balled into fists, my fingernails stabbing into my palms.

"You took a bottle of Coke," I said between clenched teeth, "and drank it before my very eyes. Here, where we are standing. You were nowhere near the bloody gate."

"No Madam, it was not me."

"I saw you do it," I screamed.

"And what's more," I went on, "I saw you trying to open the door to get inside the house!"

Then he changed tack. "Eish, Madam, I not understand what you say."

That *really* got to me. It's the biggest wonder that I didn't bop him there and then.

In no dulcet tones I told him not to give me that crap. I told him he understood perfectly, but if he didn't I'd be happy to call the police so *they* could interpret for him.

I left Ziggy guarding the guard and stormed off to phone the Security Section at Rhinestone.

I miraculously got through to Rhinestone and asked to speak to the person in charge of security. I had to word this request in several different ways, each time the only thing the dumb guy on the other end of the phone could say was, "Sorry?"

Eventually someone else came to the phone. I assumed it was the person who was purported to be in charge of this picnic, by which time I was ready to scream.

I advised him that the 'security guard' who was supposed to be protecting our property was stealing from us and had tried to force his way into our house and that I wanted something done about it.

Silence.

"We have a Rhinestone guard here and we have just caught him stealing. What are you going to do about it?"

Silence.

"Do you understand what I am saying?"

"Yes."

"Well, what are you going to do about it?"

Silence.

I then asked, "What time will the Security Chief be in the office?"

"I don't know."

"So what are you going to do about it?"

Silence.

"Shall I call the police?"

"No."

By now I was getting quite irritated and testy.

"WE HAVE A THIEF HERE UNDER THE GUISE OF BEING A RHINESTONE GUARD. WHAT DO YOU INTEND TO DO ABOUT IT?"

I think the word 'guise' threw him completely, because there was total silence again.

"Okay, okay, forget it. I shall just call the police," I yelled and slammed down the phone.

End of 'conversation' with the Rhinestone Security Department. What a bloody waste of time that was.

Ziggy came back inside, obviously having heard the tail-end of my diatribe.

"Don't waste your time phoning the police. They finish work at five o'clock."

I duly gave up.

We went back to bed, but after half an hour of all this rubbish still raging through my head I sat up and read until about half past three. I eventually managed to get some sleep but when I had to get up at 7:30 I felt totally knackered.

Ziggy went into Head Office that morning and lodged an official complaint with Rhinestone's Security Department – copying it in to all the top people, to make sure it was noted and followed up.

This probably just resulted in some other poor Rhinestone employee being allocated the thieving guard.

31

May 1981

Hello Nancy, Mev & Doris,

Two letters within a week? What is this? Have you nothing better to do? Not that I'm complaining, oh dear, no, no.

In answer to your questions:

First question: Brad's hearing has got a little better since taking a cough medicine (?) which Dr Campbell prescribed, so we don't anticipate having to rush him anywhere. However, she did say that the nature of his condition 'comes and goes' so this could be one of those 'goes' periods.

I also took Brad for a check-up to the hospital with the gynaecologist, Dr Rolph, who says that he is very pleased to say that he believes Brad has completely recovered from a strep throat/rheumatic fever problem, with no after effects.

Oops, just realised that Brad went to the paediatrician not a gynaecologist, just as well really, given that he is a boy. I always get these medical names mixed up.

Second question: Yes we are still feeding those stinking fish and that revolting chicken muck to the dogs.

On the subject of dog food I should tell you the tale of the exploding chicken stuff.

Nandy telephoned me to let me know he was off to buy some chickens. I still had several in my freezer so was in no rush for any more. However, I was almost out of dog food, so asked him to pick up a load of the chicken dog-food packs for me whilst he was there.

This he duly did and upon meeting up at the Club we transferred the large plastic sack containing approximately 50 packets from Nandy's Landcruiser into the boot of my car.

One drink led to another, as it does, and three hours later I returned home. I immediately asked Hollins to unload the stuff from my car as he was about to go off duty.

He (wisely) put the sack into the utility sink by the kitchen and beat a hasty retreat.

I wondered why he was in such a particular rush to leave – then found out. It would appear that in the heat of the boot the contents had ripened and expanded and had exploded out of their individual plastic bags into one huge mush of stuff. I say 'mush' but it was quite more varied than that.

Those little bags had contained the most gruesome combination of chicken-bits that I have ever seen in my life.

It consisted almost entirely of feet, beaks and eyeballs. I mean – there was now a sinkful of eyeballs glaring up at me! Urgh.

Despite there being little in the way of giblets, you know, necks, hearts, lungs, gizzards, etc., this conglomeration of poultry parts was still remarkably slimy.

There was no way it could be stored in the freezer en masse so I had no choice but to use my precious, rarely available, freezer bags to re-pack the bloody stuff. And I had to do it all myself. By hand.

I do not think, dear reader, you could possibly, even in your wildest nightmares, imagine what a horrendously nauseating experience that was.

As the eyeballs slithered and slipped between my fingers, the beaks and feet stabbed me. I tried wearing plastic bags on my hands, like gloves, but the eyeballs slipped inside. I found a couple of elastic bands and put them around my wrists to keep the eyeballs out but in no time at all the claws ripped the bags open anyway.

This re-packing procedure took me over an hour to complete, by which time the foul, fowl stink had increased fourfold. I dared not dwell on what it would have been like had it been the middle of summer.

And those poor workers up at the chicken farm have to deal with this on a daily basis. I still shudder at the thought.

Third Question: Has my sewing machine cooled down yet?
No. Yesterday Ziggy was later than usual going to work, so I thumbed a lift into town with him to have a casual wander around the shops. I went into a few places I'd not been into for a while and some I'd never been in at all. I discovered some very nice, reasonably priced material, so bought enough to make two dresses to sell.

I arranged for Ziggy to collect me from outside the bank at 10. He pitched at half past, which wasn't too bad for him. However, he had to 'nip back to work' for something, so I went with him.

I was given a tour of the mine – or at least the outside bits of it. We went by the smelter, acid plant and the oxygen plant (which was incredibly noisy for saying it's just air) before arriving at the 'capital holdings plant' where he had arranged to pick up some piping for the Club swimming pool. It was actually a very interesting tour.

By now it was 12:00, so we stopped at the Club for a
bite to eat. I left Ziggy there whilst I drove home,
gathered scissors, pins, needles, swimming gear and kids,
(when they'd been dropped off by the minibus) then
bundled everything and everyone into the car before
returning to the Club.

After the kiddiewinkies had had a swim and a bite to
eat and were settled happily in the playground, I set
myself up in the Copper Bar at a table to cut out the two
dresses. I was using an old dress pattern, which was
originally for a mini. All I needed to do was add several
inches to the length.

I cut out the back and then the front, but got
distracted by something in between and forgot to add the
extra inches to the front section. I could have cried.
But I didn't. I swore at myself instead.

Unfortunately a Club cleaner was walking past and
thought I was swearing at him. It took me ages to
convince him that I wasn't.

The only solution was to add a frill to the hemline to
achieve the length, but then there wasn't enough fabric
left for the second dress. I cursed some more.

Fourth Question: The kids are fine. In fact the
Terrible Trio have latched onto a new game. They pile
into the wheelbarrow — sometimes complete with Cokey —
and persuade Jackman the gardener to push them all over
the garden, which he does, at GREAT speed. He has them
screaming with delight as he winds his way around the
trees at a precarious angle. How the dog stays in without
being able to hold on is quite beyond me. It is hilarious
to watch.

You will have gathered by now that we were quite involved with film night. Not only did Ziggy work in the projection room on a Sunday, it reached the point where he also chose the film and collected it, together with any advertising posters, from the supplier. And it became incumbent upon me to sell the cinema tickets.

This particular week we were showing *Pat Garrett and Billy the Kid*. It was reckoned to be a good film and had in fact only been shown three times in Zambia, so Ziggy was quite proud of getting hold of it. This low usage being the case, it was in excellent condition which is more than could be said for some of the other films we'd shown, which jumped and juddered throughout, with lousy sound.

The films usually consisted of three reels which had to be changed over and there was normally someone helping him, to hasten the process. On this occasion there was only Ziggy and I in the projection room watching the film (or otherwise entertaining ourselves).

I had watched him change the first reel to the second, so when it came time for the final reel, I asked if I could help, as I felt confident I could handle the one end of it.

As the second reel neared conclusion I took the next one out of the box and went to put it on the projector.

"That's not the right reel." said Ziggy picking up the other reel on the desk.

"It's this one."

At which point he decided it was better to do it by himself.

However when he came to thread it, the sprockets in the celluloid were on the wrong side.

"Stupid sods," he muttered. "The last people to use it must have put a twist in the film when they rewound it."

So *he* put a twist in it and wound it back.

Whilst he was doing this I said that I thought that he would then have to wind it back again, to get to the beginning, because if someone had 'rewound it' at a twist, then he would now be starting the reel at the end rather that at the beginning.

For some reason Ziggy couldn't see what I meant. Until he tried to thread the film through the projector and found it wouldn't go.

He duly re-rewound it and finally the sprockets were in the right place. House-lights were dimmed and off we went to show the final reel of the film.

The picture came on the screen upside-down … and back to front!

What on earth was going on? We were utterly baffled.

I went into the auditorium and told the amazingly patient but somewhat confused audience that we had 'a slight technical problem' and they could go for a ten minute beer break whilst we sorted the bloody mess out.

By now there were about 20 'experts' crammed into the tiny projection room, all offering advice on what was wrong and how to put it right.

Ziggy re-wound the film, on the twist yet again and then ran it to see what was going to be there. It was the beginning of Reel ONE!

When I had passed the third reel to him it *had* been the correct reel. He was the one who had picked up Reel One which of course he had not got around to re-winding yet, so it was arse-about-face when he had tried to use it.

Talk about red faces, although we did keep the reason for the botch-up as quiet as possible.

Naturally *I* got the blame for 'interfering'. Hah!

June 1981
Dear All,
*   We have had such a hectic time of late that I don't know quite where to start. Maybe somewhere near the beginning would be good. I'm getting the distinct feeling that this letter will not be a short one.*

The first event was a cocktail party.

Each year in early June Kitwe hosts The Copperbelt Agricultural and Commercial Show. This is held at the Agricultural Showgrounds, a permanent fixture on the southern side of Kitwe.

I have no idea who was hosting the cocktail party, or how we came to get invited, but we had fun trying to find it.

Locating the Showgrounds was no problem, but once inside we didn't have a clue where to go. It turned out to be quite a big place, with what seemed like hundreds of stands. These were mostly independent brick-built structures with corrugated roofs, varying in size from a small bathroom to a car showroom, though that was not their contents, as far as we knew.

We decided to play it smart and followed two other cars who looked like they knew where they were going. After much twisting and turning we discovered that they did, they were exhibitors making their way to their own stands.

We went back to the entrance and started again. Eventually we found the place and had quite a decent time.

I had my first plastic whisky! I think Nancy said she had one on her flight over from England.

They were like IcePops, but instead of being filled with pop they contained whisky, gin or brandy and were obviously not frozen. An interesting concept for a hot day, but I was told it's not possible as alcohol does not freeze.

On Thursday night we went out for supper with Jack, who is Ziggy's mine-employed counterpart on site, to the Pink Zebra and had a very nice meal. On Friday I went to the theatre to watch the two One-Act Plays that Ziggy was Front-of-House-ing for and to be honest I wasn't too impressed. On discussion with the producer later, she said the actors had given a pathetic performance compared with that of the previous weekend. Let us just say that it was an experience I hope not to repeat.

Then came Saturday.

Saturday was the day we had arranged to take the kids to the Agricultural

Show. We went to the Club first, only to be told by Blackie it was the worst day we could choose to go, as it would be jam-packed with people who would be full of booze due to having been paid the day before.

He also warned that as well as the drunks, there would be plenty of pickpockets around. All in all, a very sunny picture was painted.

Ziggy said we should rather take them on Sunday morning but was I expected to explain to these three and four-year-olds that the event they've been looking forward to all week, and which we were on our way to, wasn't going to happen? So we went.

It was only then that the Lord and Master had the audacity to announce that he would be helping Nandy out in his Casino, so I'd be stuck with humping the clan around the showgrounds all by myself. Nice one Ziggy!

I thought about aborting the entire project, then considered again the whinging and whining that I'd have to contend with and finally decided that we'd all go along together, but when I'd had enough of it, I would take the kids home in the car. How Ziggy got home was his problem.

Perhaps I should enlarge on the Nandy casino thing.

Nandy had all the appropriate gear to run a proper but portable casino. Full-on blackjack and craps tables and a very impressive roulette table, plus hundreds of chips and everything that goes with the whole deal.

He was doing this session at the Agricultural Show as a fund-raiser for charity but he wanted to make it very professional and had asked mates to help out.

Ziggy was to be his deputy and keep a general eye on proceedings. Nandy also organised some 'bouncers', both whities and blacks, to make sure those without complementary tickets paid their K2 entrance fee and to keep any riff-raff under control or out. All these assistants were instructed to wear suits, white shirts and dicky-bows. Unbeknown to me, Ziggy had packed his formal wear into a suit carrier which he'd quietly secreted in the boot.

There was no question about it, I was running this show solo.

For security purposes I had made a point of not taking a handbag, so split my money between the two front pockets in my jeans.

Leaving Ziggy playing the boss man at the casino we went first to the main arena. It was so crowded that we had to go to the farthest end to see anything. The kids clambered up an eight-foot chain-link fence to to see over the crowd whilst I stood behind, keeping my hands over my pockets.

The action in the arena at the time was a motorcycle stunt team, one member of which was only five years old and riding a mini bike. Immediately on hearing this, all of my three wanted to have a ride on it, so I decided it was time to move on.

The only other thing that attracted their attention was a miniature train which did a circuit of the showgrounds. It actually looked like it could be quite fun for them, but was absolutely packed with *picanins* (young children).

I couldn't risk letting my three go on it on their own and I certainly didn't fancy being crammed into a tiny carriage with my three and over a hundred other excited children. Somehow I managed to dissuade them from participating in this attraction and instead headed for a bite to eat.

There was a snack bar right next door to the casino which Ziggy reckoned was okay, so I went to see what they had. Not a lot!

I ordered two beef-burgers, which didn't turn out to be quite what I expected. Each beef 'burger' consisted of a piece of steak inside a bun with sliced tomato and onion on top. The only way the kids were able to get their teeth through these was for me to take the steaks out of the buns, cut them into strips and pretend it was biltong. This we ate with half a bun each and the bits of tomato and onion on the side. It was not a particularly appetising meal but it sufficed.

Whilst this was going on, dozens of Zambian children were walking past, watching to see if we left anything.

We did a bit more wandering around before I elected to check out a childminding place we'd passed earlier, with swings, slides and climbing frames.

I plied them with ice creams and left them there, for a miniscule fee per child 'for as long as you like' (could this be days or weeks? I wondered) and headed back towards the casino and some modicum of sanity. The only downside of this was that I was not interested in gambling. After 50 minutes I had had enough (for this read 'bored stupid') so went to collect my offspring.

Along the way I came across a candy floss stall and having loved the stuff since I was a kid I decided to treat myself.

I fished out some change from my pocket and replaced the Kwacha notes. I handed over my money and as I moved to the side of the stall to collect the candy floss I felt a movement by my side. I looked down to see a black arm protruding from my left pocket!

"Get your filthy bloody thieving hand out of my pocket," I screamed.

I was going to leave it at that, then I thought, *What are you? Woman or Mouse?*

So I turned to the owner of the offending limb – a young teenager – and gave him a very hefty kick on the shin. Having enjoyed that, I decided to sock him in the face too, but was too late as he'd disappeared faster than the last cupcake at a kids' party.

Whilst being annoyed that I hadn't done more damage I was satisfied that he hadn't got off scot-free. Luckily all my money was still intact.

From there I took a slow stroll back to the crèche, keeping my right hand holding the candy floss down by my right pocket and a close watch on my other pocket whilst I used my left hand to pick and transfer the floss to my mouth.

Out of the corner of my eye I noticed another kid following me, just to my left.

When I walked faster, so did he. When I slowed down, so did he. This went on for a while. His intentions were obvious, but he eventually noticed that I was on to him and went in search of an easier target. If I had not almost been caught out earlier, I might have been nobbled by this little bugger as well. The sad thing was, this child could not have been more than seven or eight years old.

Once I had collected the kids, we returned to the candy floss stall to buy some for them and another one for me. Well, you have to make the most of these things whilst you can.

This time I stood on the ice cream side of the stall which wasn't so busy. When I asked for floss the vendor said, "Candy floss on the other side."

"I'm not going over there," said I. "The last time I did I almost had my pocket picked!"

He brought the candy floss to where we stood.

I could see that he was well aware of the problem, because every now and again he'd pick up a huge stick from under his counter and take a swift sweep across the heads of the penniless *piccanins* who crowded around his stall.

We eventually left at 5:30 and I took the kids home for some decent food before bathing and putting them to bed.

Then Hollins arrived ready to babysit whilst we went to a party at Margaret and Gordon's place.

After getting myself showered and glamified I returned to the Club to find that Ziggy had finally turned up. Within half an hour we were at Margaret and Gordon's, where we enjoyed some very nice beef stroganoff, which for me made a wonderful change from curry.

We danced for a while and then sat down. That was a big mistake as we almost fell asleep on their settee, so we left at about midnight before our lack of sociability could become an embarrassment.

It was quite disappointing really, as the party apparently went on for a couple more hours and under other circumstances (i.e. not being knackered from the day's activities) we would have thoroughly enjoyed staying longer, but Ziggy still had to drive Hollins back to his compound after we got in. Thus ended Saturday.

33

Later than intended in June 1981
Hello,

I think the next episode of our tumultuous lives will take quite some explaining.

Despite an already hectic weekend, we still had to do our Sunday stint for film night, which fortunately went without incident. However, before we left home, Chilache, our new night guard, had come to speak to me.

"Ehh, Madam, I have a problem."

He told me that his five year old daughter had gone missing from the Showgrounds on Saturday. His family assumed she was on the bus home after the event but she wasn't and no-one knew where she was. He said that if she hadn't been found by Monday lunchtime he would have to go into Rhinestone offices to try to arrange to take time off to look for her.

He actually seemed remarkably blasé about it, as if this sort of thing was only to be expected. He didn't make any mention of reporting her disappearance to the police. I wished him luck and told him to make sure he asked Rhinestone to send another guard to stand in for him if he did need time off.

Seven thirty on the Monday morning dawned bright and clear. Certainly clear of any workers. There was no sign of Hollins or Jackman. I wasn't too surprised about Hollins as when he finished babysitting on Sunday night he had complained of aching bones. However, he eventually arrived at 9:30 saying he felt even worse with a sore throat and I duly gave him a letter to take to his local clinic, asking them to sort him out. He advised that he would return to work as soon as he felt well enough.

Shortly thereafter, Jackman appeared at the gate. He also said he was not well. The previous week he had been moaning about leg pains and I had given him a note to go to the government clinic to get treated for that. Now he said he had been vomiting. Though any link between leg pains and vomiting was beyond my comprehension, I asked him if he'd been to the clinic already. He confirmed that he had and said he didn't feel up to working and left.

Half an hour later he returned, stating that he had left his ID Book in the *kaya* and needed to collect it. He reckoned there were police checks going on in the compound where he stayed so he may need it. It all sounded odd to me, but what did I know of these things?

To complete the hat trick, Chilache didn't arrive for his guard duties that night either.

I had been advised on several occasions not to keep both dogs outside at night. The well-seasoned expats of Kitwe explained that they could be distracted by potential burglars or even, heaven forbid, poisoned. I had taken no notice of this in the past, having the benefit of Rhinestone's efficient security and all.

However since the occasion of the thieving relief night guard their reliability had come into question and I decided to keep Cokey in at night, given that his size was hardly a deterrent to burglars. But if he were inside and heard something going on outside whilst our guard was getting his head bashed in or perhaps taking a nap, Coke might at least bark before anyone got the chance to break into the house and poison him.

Tuesday morning arrived, but unfortunately Hollins and Jackman did not. I did some sewing and in the afternoon took the kids to the Club for a swim.

I took the precaution of putting on the outside house-lights before leaving, in case we returned after it got dark. (Sharp thinker, me.) We returned home at 6:30, had a bite to eat and put the kids to bed. After reading my book for a while I cleared off to bed at about 10:00 and Ziggy joined me after about thirty minutes.

Before you continue with this tale, dear reader, you may want to refer to page 25 showing the floor-plan of our house. It could make what I am about to describe a little more comprehensible.

I was getting rather neurotic about sounds in the night ever since our experience with the guard trying to get into the kitchen. Several nights I had woken up thinking I'd heard noises only to find nothing of consequence.

This night I woke up with a start, just after midnight.

Although I had been sound asleep an inner voice said something dramatic had awakened me. A familiar noise, in fact.

When we first moved into McFrazier Crescent, and Vicki and Leon were slightly smaller, they were unable to open the back door from outside because the handle was too high for them to reach. They got into the habit of thumping it, or bashing it with their bums when they wanted to come in.

As I delved into my subconscious I was sure the noise that suddenly woke me had sounded just like that.

I lay in bed hardly daring to breath and prayed that Ziggy didn't start to snore and 'get in the way of' my auditory scrutiny.

This may sound stupid, but I have found that when I try to listen to some distinct noise I need to keep my eyes open. I listened for quite a while but my eyes began to close and I could feel myself drifting back to sleep.

Fortunately, just before I drifted off I heard another abnormal sound. That perked me up again and I returned to my vigilant audial focus.

The noise I heard sounded a bit like rustling and then it dawned on me. With Hollins not being at work for the past couple of days, the rubbish bin in the kitchen hadn't been emptied since Saturday. It was full of papers and cardboard rubbish that I'd made the kids clear up from their bedrooms, as well as other rubbish.

Obviously the puppy was ferreting about in the bin. I imagined the mess which could be made by all this stuff being scattered across the kitchen floor. The little sod.

As I lay there wondering whether or not I could be bothered to go and kick his arse and put him outside, I heard an odd sounding clunk and decided that I had perhaps better go and investigate.

As I reached the bedroom door I could still hear rustling. Rather a lot of rustling for such a small dog, in fact. Now I was a little worried. Ziggy was the last one to bed, so I wasn't sure if he had closed the door which connects the bedroom passage to the living area. What if it was open and it wasn't the dog making the noise?

Snapping myself out of this state of mind I slowly and carefully opened the bedroom door and peeked around it. Thankfully the passage door was shut. I crept out of the bedroom and took three paces to the door where I stood listening again.

I could still hear 'sounds' but then heard what seemed like walking noises. And to be honest, it did not sound like a walking dog.

By this time my heart was beginning to pound somewhat.

I heard Cokey whine, like he does when he wants to be let out at night. He continued to whine. But it was rather early for his 'wee break'. So what was he whining about?

This clearly warranted some further investigation, but I was very reluctant to open that passage door. Then I had a brainwave.

There were no lights on in the bedroom corridors so I could walk down to the far end, by Vicki's bedroom, and peer through the window which looks out onto the back yard. From there I should be able to see across to the back door (you remember - it was that 'back door bashing sound' that woke me) or see if any intruders were in evidence in the yard.

I began to creep down the passage.

When I was but a stripling, my leg joints used to click and creak if I tried to creep around quietly. It must be something to do with tension because sod my luck if they suddenly didn't start up now!

So I clicked and creaked my way along the passageway and turned right into the section where Vicki's bedroom was, taking me to the rear, yard-facing window.

Crouched and moving forward I ducked below the level of the window.

Very, very slowly I turned and eased myself until I could peer through the glass. There was no sign of anyone in the yard. Phew, relief. I stood up and let my gaze drift towards the rear wall.

I thought it was my imagination at first, but when I moved to the furthest section of the window I could clearly see the back of the house.

My heart came into my mouth and my stomach disappeared somewhere down into my ankles. The back door *was* open!

At that point I nearly sh*t myself.

My knees went weak, I started to shake, and I stopped breathing.

It was only as I stood resolutely taking deep breaths and trying to calm myself that I looked down and realised I was standing there stark naked. In my single-minded determination to play amateur sleuth I had forgotten to put on any clothes.

Between me and the relative safety of my bedroom was a considerable expanse of corridor, which led up to an *unlocked door* (there was no key for it), on the other side of which there was an unknown quantity of burglars. I was terrified.

Drawing a deep breath and holding it for dear life I dashed, as much as one could with jelly legs and percussion joints, back to the bedroom. The only positive aspect was that my bare feet made no noise and the bedroom door had been left open.

Once back in the bedroom I almost collapsed with relief and didn't think I would be able to speak properly in my continued non-breathing, shaking state.

Ziggy could sleep through an earthquake, and given the trouble I had rousing him when the guard was up the tree, I didn't hold out much hope for co-operation.

I moved to the bed and put my hands on his shoulders. With my mouth close enough to his ear to taste the earwax, I whispered, "Ziggy, there's someone in the kitchen."

There must have been something in my voice which registered that this was serious because he shot bolt upright and (thankfully) whispered, "What?"

I hastily and quietly explained to him what had woken me up and what I had done since.

He leapt out of bed silently, pulled on a pair of shorts and headed for the door.

I was terrified that he would barge in on the burglar/s and get attacked. I hastily found my green corduroy overalls and dragged them on before following him. In hindsight that was an awesomely stupid move, but in a situation like that you don't think too clearly.

By the time I'd got the bib straps over my shoulders, Ziggy had already opened the passage door and seeing nobody there went into the kitchen.

I joined him as he was coming back out brandishing our huge steel chef's knife and raced towards the lounge, where the main light was on.

He came out, shouting, "What a bastard!" and flew into the dining room, switching on the light in there.

We immediately saw that one of the windows was wide open. There was a small amount of broken glass on the floor and the burglar bars were cut and wrenched up inside, almost to the ceiling.

Turning on our heels we tore out through the back door and down the drive to see someone's legs disappearing over the garden wall. As we got closer we could see they (it was obvious there was more than one) had put one of our wooden garden benches against the wall to aid their escape.

Ziggy leapt onto the bench and leaning over the wall yelled, louder than I had ever heard him shout before, "You Bastards!"

I tore back up to the house, grabbed the axe from the broom cupboard and my house keys to unlock the gate and raced after Ziggy.

"Let's go get 'em," I yelled.

We charged out of the gate, with Ziggy wielding his knife and me waving the wood axe around my head like something demented.

We stood on the edge of the *vlei* across the road.

"You thieving bloody kaffirs," I screamed, using the 'K' word I had vowed *never* to use.

Ziggy shouted, "You bastards!" over and over.

Both of us behaved like a pair of raving lunatics. With all this screaming and shouting going on, every dog for about six blocks around (except ours, of course) was barking like crazy.

Then we heard sounds of movement in a bush nearby, but before we could reach it, the thieving bastard managed to run off into the *vlei*. However, there we were lucky enough to discover behind the bush the cassette player, one of the large Onyo speakers and my wicker basket – stuffed full with a variety of goodies.

The next move was to get the car, so Ziggy fetched the car keys and tore off down McFrazier Road whilst I stood over the recovered loot wielding my axe.

It was only at this moment that I looked down, to see that my attire for this venture was not entirely appropriate. Or fitting to be more precise.

Wearing only the corduroy overalls, my tits were sticking out either side of the bib like a pair of puppies peeking out from behind a pillar. Thank goodness the thieves had been running in the opposite direction. The mind boggles at what a sight my far from petite, bouncing boobs presented as I tore down the drive screaming like a banshee and waving my axe.

Having achieved the square root of sod-all Ziggy returned in the car. I gathered up the rescued paraphernalia and hastened inside to make myself more decent.

I suggested to Ziggy that we get hold of a load of guys from work to help track the bastards down. Unfortunately none of them were on the phone. [This was centuries before cell phones existed.]

So I called Molly and after waking her up and explaining the situation, asked her if Doug could go to their apartment blocks and alert the guys (Blackie, John, Terry, Tony, Andy, Roger, etc., etc.) to our situation and ask them to come and help in the search.

I then phoned Gordon to ask if he could help whilst we waited for the Rhinestone reinforcements.

Gordon and I, and a Land Rover full of lads he'd got hold of, circled the waste ground with the Landy's lights off, then blasted them full on in the hope of seeing some signs of movement. More troops arrived and we had the place totally surrounded.

We travelled every road and cul de sac in the area, several of the guys went *bundu* bashing into the *vlei*, checking out deep ditches and sturdy bushes which might conceal a dark body or stashed swag but found nothing or nobody.

After half an hour they'd had absolutely no luck in tracking the burglars down so the posse returned home to their beds, no doubt cursing us for disturbing their sleep.

In the meantime, Doug had made himself doubly useful by getting through to the Rhinestone offices and organising a security guard whom he knew to be reliable because we had been left with a wide open window and a kitchen door we could no longer lock.

By now it was about 3 am. Ziggy went off for another drive around the streets whilst I stayed at home. Vicki and Leon had woken up, obviously from all the commotion and it was almost four o'clock by the time I got them back to bed.

Ziggy and I eventually went for a lie down as we were absolutely shattered. We agreed to get up pre-dawn to see if any abandoned items could be sighted in the cold light of day, so that we might retrieve more of our possessions before someone else came across them.

At the first signs of the dawn light I donned some warm clothes and went and climbed a tree immediately across the road to get a better view of the area and what did I find?

Not a bloody thing.

The burglars had got away with: the hi-fi turntable and amplifier, my purse with its contents, a hold-all containing towels and swimming gear, and my sewing machine! AND they had wrapped their booty in our dining room curtains for easy portage!

In the basket which we had managed to recover was: our iron, two tablecloths, my sewing box, box of sewing machine bobbins, a shirt I had almost finished making for Brad, two I was in the middle of for Vicki and

Leon, K24 worth of material and my empty, apart from a hairbrush, handbag.

Included on the missing-list from my bag was my English driving license and Burton on Trent library card. Like that would be really useful to someone living in Zambia!

But, oh dear, what a pity, what a shame... They didn't get the power cable and pedal for the sewing machine which was a make only available in the UK. Also the turntable and amp had very unusual socketry, so the only things of any use they were left with were the curtains and the swimming stuff. I hoped they would drown.

34

Dear Nancy, Mev & Doris,
Do you remember that when I was a kid I wanted to be a policeman — well, policewoman actually.
This was my chance to turn detective.

On checking the dining-room window, we found that the shattered glass lay mostly on the outside. And the burglar bars were forced open and bent upwards on the inside. A very difficult manoeuvre if you had been outside the window.

Then we checked the back door.

The marks on the door indicated that it had been forced open from the *inside*. Thus, the only conclusion was that someone had entered with a key, re-locked the door and then forced the door open later to make it look like a break-in.

Obviously the breaking open of the dining-room window was to provide them with another escape route. We began to realise this was a very well-orchestrated plan.

They must have left the false break-in of the back door until they were getting ready to leave, because after I was woken by the back door noise they would not have had time to:
- extricate the stereo from the wall cupboard
- remove the curtains in the manner they had - hook by hook
- break open the burglar bars from the inside
- go through the cupboards where the table cloths were kept, and they were *very* selective about what they took from there
- sort through the contents of my handbag
- load all the loose stuff into the basket; and then sod off with all their booty

There was only one person who knew the layout of the place, exactly where everything would be and had a key to our back door. Hollins.

Hollins appeared on the scene at about 8am that morning whilst I was getting the kids dressed for school. They had all been fed, but I was trying to get drinks and biscuits into boxes, wash faces, comb hair, etc.

All this time Hollins just stood in the kitchen watching the proceedings with the most idiotic look on his face, as if he were about to start crying. I eventually got so pissed off that I asked him,

"Have you come to do any work today?"

He held up his arms in an attitude of questioning disbelief and said

"Yes, Madam," and pointing at the window asked, "but what?"

For pity's sake.

I shouted "What on earth do you think has happened? Some thieving swines have broken in and stolen our stuff."

At which point I walked away in disgust, herding the kids to the bus, which had been patiently waiting for fifteen minutes.

When I returned to the kitchen he still hadn't moved, but was looking at the stack of dishes waiting to be washed. I said he should forget about that for now and do the laundry which had piled up since he had been 'off sick'.

On Wednesday afternoon Ziggy went to the local police station to report the incident. The fact that I had phoned them an hour after it happened appeared not to have been registered by anyone.

They said they would send someone round to look at the crime scene. Nobody came.

Ziggy went to the site and collected David, the Rhinestone carpenter. He fitted a new lock to the back door. Then he spent several days with us replacing all the remaining locks so every door to every room or passageway or store cupboard was lockable. I finished up with a bunch of 19 different keys, plus duplicates.

Ziggy planned to go and talk to someone in CID, to ask them to question Hollins, Jackman and the guard, but after listening to other people, he didn't anticipate much success.

Over the next few days the atmosphere in the house when Hollins was working was somewhat strained. Without having actually accused him, the vibes bouncing off the walls were not good.

Of Jackman there was no sign at all. The issue of him returning to collect his registration card when he was 'sick' seemed to indicate he had no intention of coming back to work.

The following Saturday Hollins arrived late for work and proceeded to give me some cockamamie crap about Jackman having stolen his record player when it was at a repair shop.

The whole story was so elaborately inventive it was very evident to me that Hollins was trying to put Jackman in a bad light and himself as a hapless victim, similar to us and our burglary.

I might be a bit stupid down one side on a Thursday, but his cock and bull story did not wash with me. I showed little interest in his ramblings and told him just to get on with the job for which he was being paid.

I had been having considerable trouble with him not getting on with his work. I was so angry that one day I said if he couldn't do the job I would find someone else who could. It seemed obvious to me that he was being intentionally slow, almost as if he wanted to get the sack.

I had already decided he was going to get it, but only after he had caught up with all his chores as I did not want to get stuck with yet another mountain of ironing like I had in December.

It was when looking at the ironing waiting to be done that I thought there were some things missing.

Several days after the burglary we had been going somewhere special and I tried to track down a pair of T-shirts for Vicki and Leon to wear.

Whilst I didn't often dress them alike, on odd occasions I would put them in matching T-shirts, with Leon in shorts and Vicki in a skirt. I could make most of their clothes but not T-shirts, so when buying those I would get two or sometimes three of the same design.

Despite a thorough check I could now find only one T-shirt. That started buzzers and alarm bells ringing in my head.

The next day I searched everywhere; the dirty laundry basket, the 'waiting to be ironed' basket and their wardrobes.

Of every single T-shirt we had duplicated (at least ten), we now had only one of each.

I continued the search to see what else was missing. The list was substantial.

Hollins could try to blame Jackman for stealing some items from the washing line, but only Hollins would know which T-shirts were duplicated as they were rarely worn (and therefore washed) on the same day.

Then I checked my wardrobe and found six pairs of knickers to be missing. That was particularly odd because on the advice of Molly I had always washed my own brookies (as they were called there). *Those* could not have been stolen from the washing line because I always hung them to dry inside the bathroom.

The finger now seriously pointed at Hollins and whilst I doubted we could prove it, it sealed his fate as far as I was concerned.

The next Saturday morning I went to open the gates for Ziggy to go to work, when there was a voice on the other side.

"Good Morning, Madam."

Good Grief. There stood Jackman, large as life.

Ziggy reversed down the drive.

"Never a dull moment, is there?" I muttered to him.

Once inside the gates Jackman went off at a tangent to explain why he had not been to work, saying he'd gone with a man to get Hollins's record player (which he strangely assumed I knew all about) and that the man and some other men, had set upon him and beaten him up.

He tried to show me wounds on his knees, legs and arms, although I only saw one small graze on his knee. He said since the attack he had been recovering from his injuries and attempting to track down the record player.

I suppose it was sheer coincidence that he returned to work on pay day.

I asked him if he had come to work. He said that he had, but before going to get changed into his overalls he asked me if Hollins was here.

"No." I answered "Have you seen him lately?"

He replied that he had not.

"Then things should get interesting when Hollins arrives," I muttered under my breath as he walked away.

Five minutes later Jackman came to me asking for the gate key to let Hollins in.

The two then walked up to the kitchen and standing right outside the door, commenced an argument. Now if that wasn't contrived then my nose is a carrot.

When they have held conversations in the past they've spoken to each other in Bemba, but this argument was being conducted in English, obviously for my benefit. And it would have been far more normal if they had argued at the bottom of the driveway, or even in the *kaya*, but there they stood, right outside the kitchen shouting at each other so that I could hear every word.

Eventually I put a stop to the nonsense by telling both of them to shut up and get on with some work. I was furious that they thought I was stupid enough to believe all that rubbish.

Contrary to his usual routine Ziggy returned home by about 10 o'clock and I filled him in on what had transpired.

"That's it then," he said. "I'll go out right now and fire Jackman. You fire Hollins at the end of his days' work."

Since we had recently lent Jackman almost a month's wages, he was hardly in a position to claim any severance pay.

After Ziggy told him his fortune, the little sh*t even had the nerve to come to me and say, "Goodbye, Madam" with a big smile on his face. He was obviously very proud that he'd got away with (a) his share in the stolen loot and (b) not having to repay the loan.

Hollins continued to work his normal Saturday shift until about 12:30 at which time I walked into the kitchen, shaking in advance of the confrontation.

"Hollins, as of now we shall no longer require your services."

He said nothing.

I told him that I wasn't happy about discovering things were missing. He still said nothing.

I said he was getting this month's wages and not a penny more.

"What about holiday pay?"

"Holiday pay? Bloody Holiday Pay? You should count yourself lucky that I'm not deducting any money from your pay for what you have stolen."

"Do you mean that you suspect me of taking things?" he asked.

I told him that too right I did and recounted exactly what I had discovered (or not) in my search through the wardrobes.

"Nobody else had the opportunity to take those things, so it could have only been you."

He said nothing.

I also said that we were suspicious of the circumstances surrounding the 'break-in' as it was obvious that the burglars had a key. I instructed him to go to the *kaya* and collect whatever possessions belonged to him and leave.

At NO time did he deny any of the accusations I made.

And that was that.

No argument, no apology, no kiss my arse or bugger-all. He left.

It had been horrible having him around when we suspected him of being involved in the break-in.

Ziggy and I then relaxed on the sofa, both feeling as if a great weight had been lifted from our shoulders.

35

July 1981
Dear All,
Our friends Pam and Chris were aware of what had been
going on with our servant problems and had asked their
houseboy Edward (the one who babysat for us at New Year)
if he knew of anyone honest and hardworking who might be
willing to work for us. He did.
The new guy started this morning and his name is
Benton. He seems to be doing okay so far, but I am not
sure if he will last; you should have seen his face when
he saw the pile of washing in the laundry bin!

Benton had arrived at 7:25 – when I was up to my eyes trying to get the tribe ready for school. Shortly afterwards David the carpenter was knocking at the gate to be let in. Then the phone rang. It was for Ziggy but he was in the shower so I had to take a message. By then Vicki's soft-boiled egg (with soldiers) was hard-boiled.

Just as I was starting to win, the bloke who'd phoned arrived, so I had to go and let *him* in.

I eventually got rid of the kids, Ziggy and his mate, and found time to give Benton a brief outline of his jobs.

I had barely got him sorted out when there was another knock at the gate. It was a woman who I had met at a Rhinestone function the day before and whom, in a moment of madness, I had invited round for coffee. I had completely forgotten about it.

She turned out to be quite nice, but for the life of me I couldn't remember her name and as she was greeting me like a long lost friend, I didn't like to ask. She and her husband (who I did remember was George) arrived a month after us, but were initially posted to work/live in Kafue, some seven hours drive south of Kitwe. They had a two-year-old daughter and were expecting another. She left at about 12:20.

But before she left, eight workers rolled up in a Rhinestone van to fix our toilet in the shower room, as it had been leaking water. I didn't know how all these workers were going to fit in there as the room wasn't that big.

This house was getting busier than Burton Bingo Hall on pension day.

Then Ziggy arrived with the kids as the school bus was out of action again. He didn't have time to stay for lunch as he'd borrowed someone else's car to fetch them as his was in for a service so had to go and pick up the guy whose car he was using. It was probably as well because during all the confusion of the day, I had forgotten to take meat out of the freezer, so we only had egg and chips.

Then half-way through lunch I received a phone call from Lou, asking if Dennis could come around to play, as she had to go to work. She and Ryan were staying in Margaret and Gordon's house whilst they were away on leave, so were only a stone's throw away. I had no problem with that anyway. When you've got three kids what's one more, especially on the sort of day I was having?

When we employed Benton we made sure that he knew the rules right from the word go by coming up with a letter of terms and conditions which we jointly signed.

Ziggy & Ann Patras
61 McFrazier Road,
Kitwe
6th July 1981
To Benton Bunda
General Guidelines for Employment
Wages: K45 per month. K2.00 weekly allowance
Kaya accommodation for employee, wife and children.
One bag of mealie will be provided each month.
Some hand soap will be provided each week.
Babysitting — K2.00 per night, payable on Saturdays.
It is not our policy to lend money at all. However, under certain circumstances an advance of K10.00 may be allowed half way through the month.
The kaya and kaya yard are to be kept thoroughly clean at all times.
The condition of the kaya may be inspected by employers at any reasonable time. Your children are to remain inside the kaya yard, unless otherwise agreed by employers.
No visitors are to be brought inside the gates unless previously agreed by employers.
Strictly NO livestock may be kept (especially chickens).
Co-operation would be appreciated in ensuring that the property is never left unoccupied during the daytime. If you know that you are all going to be out over a weekend, please let us know, so we can organise a day-guard.
You will be provided with a gate key. The gates must be kept locked at all times.
Signed _____ Benton Bunda
Signed _____ A Patras
Dated _____

That may seem quite harsh, but was the norm at the time.

Several of the 'old colonial' ex-pats had said we were too soft with our employees and intimated that was why we had been 'taken advantage of' by our previous domestics.

I still recall how horrified we were at the prospect of having servants when we first moved to Zambia, but quickly realised that there was a practical reason for the exercise. It also meant that someone had a steady job, who would otherwise be without an income. However, I was adamant that whoever worked for me would be treated in a way which did not compromise my conscience.

After spending the first week getting the chores sorted, Benton went off to somewhere remote at the weekend to fetch his wife and two children from his village and they soon settled well into life in the *kaya*.

On the subject of the *kaya*, I must tell you that I initially felt rather embarrassed by having servants living in a small building at the bottom of the garden. It consisted of only one room, and a toilet with a crude shower facility, whereas we lived in a huge house where everyone had their own bedroom, apart from all the other facilities. It seemed so demeaning to expect them to live in such cramped conditions.

It was only as we travelled out and about in more remote areas, where we could see mud and thatch villages in the distance, that I realised this was a misjudgement on my part.

Out in the bush, where they had all the space in the world, as well as plenty of natural resources for the project, they actually chose to live in incredibly small, all-in-one round huts.

Knowing that we were trying to find someone to look after our garden, Benton suggested that maybe his wife could help. So we decided to pay Catrina to do a few chores, like moving the sprinkler around, clearing up the doggy landmines and doing the odd bit of hoeing. The arrangement worked pretty well.

Whilst she was working, their kids just sat in the *kaya* yard and did nothing. This seemed quite wretched to me, but it apparently was the norm.

36

July 1981
Still Here
Dear All,

I seem to be spending all my time at this bloody typewriter lately.

I've just finished a letter to Swansea to try and replace my driving licence. I asked them to send it to you, rather than risk it getting nicked in the post here. Could you just keep it safe until we come back, please?

I still haven't got around to taking my Zambian Drivers Test, although I have had my photo taken ready for it. Oh, and I didn't tell you about Ziggy's experience(s) with his driving test. To ensure that I get this right I have asked him to recount it in his own words — but I shall do the typing, given the skills (or lack of) he previously demonstrated in that field.

Dictated by Ziggy:

In sunny ole' B-O-T not by the Sea, as in many towns in UK, driving tests bring fear into young hearts. Different instructors, cars, courses, testers….

But I'm not scared, not in Zambia.

I've been through the rigmarole of UK testing and I've been through the Advanced Driving Institute tests and the Hendon Police College High Speed Drivers Training Course. Jody Scheckter eat your heart out. Or so I thought…

Booking the test is done by my minions. Test centre just around the corner. Breeze.

Now remember I'm the Bwana Mkubwa (Big Boss). Flash car, smart clothes, my own driver, etc. So when I arrive at the test centre some sloppily dressed idiot eventually arrives and shuffles paper…

This gets up my nose. I've got work to do and I ask some 10 minutes later, not too politely, "Is there anyone in charge here?"

Mistake number one. The 'idiot' is the gentleman in charge.

And he is the one, in his own good time, of course, conducting the test.

In the UK you might touch the mirror to indicate that you're using it. Wrong. Failed. Reason — adjusting mirror whilst driving.

Second attempt. Different week, different examiner, same test course because there is only one course in Kitwe. Same car, same clothes. Second Big mistake: I asked the tester whether I should use hand signals. His reply was, "I'm only the observer."

Failed for not using hand signals. (Nothing else was on the roads at the time.)

Right, fella. With all my UK achievements, I am not going to be beaten.

Third time around I arrive at the test centre, dressed in denims, driving one of the Company pick-ups, so small you could pick it up (almost) and carry it under your arm.

This time the tester was waving to his chums in the streets instead of observing and it would seem I was just his chauffeur.

Result: Passed.

After 3 attempts !!

She -- The One Who Has To Be Obeyed — has yet to take her driving test. Let's see how <u>she</u> gets on!
Ziggy.

Next to hit the fan was when we heard that Ryan had been given the sack from work.

Apparently he had spent more time than was considered acceptable drinking at lunchtimes. He was told that if his habits persisted, serious disciplinary action would be taken.

Then one week he took some time off to make up a long weekend to go fishing, unfortunately without all the appropriate permissions. When he returned to site on the Tuesday he was given the push.

The way it affected me was that I lost a friend, so did Brad, and we adopted two more bloody dogs. In a moment of madness I agreed to take their two, on the proviso that Lou found a good, loving, allowed-inside home for the aging Brandy. I couldn't cope with four dogs. Imagine the number of doggy land-mines being doubled!

Urghh.

We still hadn't managed to replace the stereo units which were stolen so I took to listening, for the first time in Zambia, to our portable radio. I couldn't figure out what station I was listening to as all the announcements and jingles were in Italian, but the music was good (all English pop and rock).

Even above the sound of the radio, at one point I thought it had gone unusually quiet. After a quick search I found the kids ferreting about in my wardrobe. I caught the little buggers just in time. They had found a packet containing three tubes of Rowntrees Fruit Pastilles. I had forgotten all about them and as the kids had finished all their lunch and had not been giving me too much uphill, I let them enjoy the treat.

I happened to mention that I liked the black ones, so each time one of them found a black one it was proudly presented to me -- then he/she stood around and watched to see how much I enjoyed it. By the time they were finished I felt quite bilious.

Several days later...

I'm waiting for Peter to pick me up, then on to collect the kids and Ziggy, to drive us to the local puncture parlour to get ourselves up to date with cholera injections. We realised the other week that our cholera vaccination only lasts for six months and so decided that we ought to renew it. I am not looking forward to the experience.

Oh, I've just realised that I didn't tell you about Peter. He is our new designated driver and seems very nice and he's great with the kids.

Talking of whom, the school Sports Day was held last Tuesday and was absolutely hilarious.

This was our first experience of school races other than our own half a lifetime ago. I had forgotten how much fun kiddies races were and while still taken quite seriously by some budding athletes, our three weren't exactly in that league.

Leon was very inventive in the sack race. Instead of jumping awkwardly along like the other kids, resembling constipated kangaroos, he stuck a foot in each corner of the sack and proceeded to walk, very slowly, up the track. The level of concentration on his face whilst doing this was classical. When he reached the finishing line he just stood and waited there, wearing a big fat grin, for someone to come along and remove him from his sack.

Vicki on the other hand simply stood rooted to the ground at the starting line, with her face turned sideways and refused to go anywhere.

Next came Brad in the Hopping Race.

He started out hopping, fell over, then noticed the others were *way* in front of him. He ran to catch up with them, then continued to hop and came in second! Little cheat. Obviously takes after his father.

Then there was the Run Backwards race, which in Leon's case was a Walk Backwards race. But he must have really enjoyed it because later, when it came to the 20metre dash, he decided to do that one backwards too.

We had expected the Sports Day to last about an hour, but when they stopped for 'half time refreshments' at 10:30 we realised it was unlikely to finish for another hour.

Ziggy was tearing his hair out by now, as he wanted to get back to work to sort out the petty cash before the cashier left the office at 11:00, but Peter had disappeared somewhere with the car, so Ziggy couldn't go anywhere.

First after the break was the Fathers Race. Just as the dads were lined up for it (including Ziggy!) Peter returned, resulting in Ziggy racing in the opposite direction, towards the car park. On the whole it turned out to be a really good event, but once again I forgot to take the camera.

Peter was turning out to be worth his weight in gold (well copper I suppose, in that region) and wanted to work all the hours he could. We personally paid him overtime when he worked for us at home. He became our 'day guard' on a Saturday and Sunday. And rather than just sitting on his arse doing nothing , he built a fence around the kaya, to keep Benton's family safe from the dogs. Though even with the fence, they were still not allowed chickens!

His next project, was to build a fence to surround the vegetable patch.

Yes, Peter was a very useful additional to the 'family'.

So, Nancy, Mev and Doris,

I may not have time for any more letters for a while.

As it is coming up to the end of our first year here, we are going away on holiday for a couple of weeks at the end of this month, and I have a lot to do before then. I shall try and write to you once I am relaxing in a hotel.

In the meantime take care of yourselves, say hello to all the nice people we know at the pub — and watch out for rowdies, and strangers bearing gifts.

Tons of love for now,

Ann, Ziggy, Brad, Vicki & Leon

Xx xx xx xx xx

37

Well, that's it, dear reader. I have reached the end of my first year as an expatriate writing letters from Zambia, though this is not where this story ends. Oh, no.

Back at the beginning of June, Brad had been experiencing problems with his ears again. Ziggy approached Rhinestone to see if they would pay for us to take him out of the country to see a specialist and possibly have surgery for insertion of grommets. South Africa was closer and cheaper to fly to than the UK, but we knew no-one there, and would need to stay in a hotel. Ziggy pointed out that accommodation in the UK would be free, and we knew which doctors to contact there.

Not only did they agree to buy tickets for Brad and me to fly over, but knowing that they would probably get little productive work out of Ziggy if he was left in charge of Vicki and Leon in my absence, they offered to pay for all of us to go over, including Ziggy!

We couldn't believe our luck.

I immediately contacted the paediatrician (not gynaecologist!) who had cared for all our kids as babies and having explained our situation, asked if he could suggest an ENT specialist. He did and we managed to get an appointment at the beginning of August. We were impressed with the speed of this at such short notice, but then we were going 'private'.

We also made the momentous decision not to tell any of our family or friends in the UK of our forthcoming visit.

Having booked the appropriate flights I wrote to the Riverside Hotel on the outskirts of Burton, to see if they could accommodate us for the first couple of nights of our visit, until we were able to make alternative arrangements to stay with family.

A reservation was confirmed and the Reception staff and hotel owners were sworn to secrecy not to tell *anyone* about our booking, as my parents often visited the Riverside on their night off from The Burton Arms.

In Kitwe we arranged for one of Ziggy's work mates to house-sit for the duration of our trip, and were happy in the knowledge that we could safely leave Benton to continue with his duties and feed the dogs.

We succeeded in keeping news of our impending trip from the kids until the week before we were due to fly, but the final few days before our departure were sizzling with excitement.

On the 31st July (Ziggy's birthday) Peter loaded all our near-empty suitcases into the company car and drove us to Southdowns Airport. The custom of all expatriates on a trip home was to travel out with near-empty suitcases and fill them in the UK with all the essential and special items which could not be bought in Zambia. By now we were quite familiar with Southdowns Airport. It had seemed so shabby almost a year ago, but now we were quite happy to take advantage of its close proximity to commence our long journey.

The flight down to Lusaka was uneventful, as was the ten-hour long haul from Lusaka to Heathrow. This time I certainly did not waste time or patience trying to change the kids into pyjamas. *I still cannot believe I did that on the initial flight over. What an idiot I was!*

Nor were we fazed by the hustle and bustle of Heathrow airport before boarding the final leg of our long, tiring yet happy journey to East Midlands Airport.

Upon reaching EMA, which is just half an hour's drive to Burton, we piled ourselves and our baggage into an obliging taxi.

Ziggy and I had travelled this route many times over the years so it was a treat to see the regular villages and familiar hostelries looking just the same as they always had. It seemed like a lifetime ago since we had driven down those lanes.

During the journey we told the taxi driver where we had come from and how we planned to surprise our family with our unannounced arrival. He thought it was brilliant and as we drew closer was getting almost as excited as we were.

We hit Burton upon Trent and were less than half a mile from my parents' pub when Brad made an announcement.

"Mummy, I'm going to be sick."

I told him that we really were almost there, so he must just 'hold it in'.

As the taxi drew to a halt outside the Burton Arms it all came out. Yes, our little angel threw up all down the back of the driver's seat, barely missing the driver.

I couldn't believe it. Mortified, embarrassed and gagging are just a few of the words that would describe my reaction to this scene.

I apologised profusely to the taxi driver, but explained that we needed to get inside as quickly as possible before any of the regular customers saw us. There could be some mean people around who would take great delight at rushing into the pub to blab to Mev or Nancy about our unexpected arrival.

I offered to return and clean up the mess as soon as we had sprung our surprise. He was very sweet about it.

"Ah don't worry, me duck. This sort of thing is all part of being a taxi driver. And believe me, I've 'ad worse."

I was so glad I hadn't been around for that...

The timing of our arrival at 10:35 could not have been better, as The Burton Arms doors would have just been unlocked.

Whilst we had been waiting for our luggage at the airport we had prepped the kids on how we were going to accomplish our surprise. Even at their tender ages of three and four they understood completely what to do and the need for getting it just right.

We walked quietly into the pub and after peeping carefully around the bar door, where I saw my dad standing behind the bar counter with his back to us, I silently ushered the kids into the bar room.

The kids lined up side by side, waiting for a cue from me.

"HELLO, BRANBAND!" they yelled at the tops of their voices.

He stopped what he was doing with his hand poised in mid-move, much like children at a party playing musical statues. He remained rigid for several seconds before slowly turning round, his eyes as wide as beer coasters and his mouth open.

Eventually he managed to speak.

"Bloody hell!"

Once he'd collected himself he dashed round to where they stood and gave them big hugs and kisses, followed by a similar response to Ziggy and me.

He then told us that Nancy was in the kitchen preparing the pub sandwiches.

We moved quickly and quietly down the corridor.

The kitchen door was ajar and I could hear the radio playing, which was obviously why my mum had not heard the kids yelling in the bar. As I gently pushed it open I could see she too had her back to the door, as she prepared the bar snacks.

Again I let the kids creep in first and followed them. Nobody had yet said a word but, as us women so often do, she must have 'sensed' something and turned to see what, or who, it was.

Her face was an absolute picture. And she dropped her tomatoes.

She wanted to pick them all up together (the kids, not the tomatoes) but they were just too big for that now. Instead she got down on her knees and kissed and hugged them until they nearly turned blue.

Then after picking up the trampled toms, it was my turn for the hugs and kisses.

It was all just so overwhelming, she and I were both laughing and crying at the same time, with the kids jumping around us like they were attached to an invisible puppet-master by elastic.

Led by the squealing kids, we all trooped back to the bar for more hugs, kisses and tears of delight.

In the meantime Ziggy and the taxi driver had offloaded our luggage. The driver was leaning against the bar with a big grin on his face, delighted to be a part of this celebration, saying, "Cheers" to everyone with his glass of lemonade.

After calming down with suitable refreshments I had to concede to the kids' – Leon's in particular – cries to "go and find Nannan."

We trouped up the stairs to the pub living quarters to find Doris who, being a late riser, was still sleep.

She was absolutely stunned and thrilled to be raucously awakened by her three favourite great-grandchildren who instantly leapt onto the bed to play 'All Pile On Nannan'.

It was a damn good job no-one in my family suffered from a weak heart or this sudden shock could have had disastrous consequences.

We have always been a family who love surprises and this was truly the very best we had EVER achieved.

Two days after our arrival in Burton we took Brad along to see the ENT Specialist, and after an examination he concurred with the Zambian doctor's diagnosis and proposed treatment. An appropriate operation for the insertion of grommets was scheduled for the following week. We were advised that Brad should be fit to fly back to Zambia after he'd had a check-up a week following his op.

Unfortunately Ziggy couldn't stay with us that long, as his site managerial skills were being sorely missed in Zambia, so he flew back at the end of two weeks.

The children loved their three week holiday in England and all were spoilt absolutely rotten by their grandparents, aunts, uncles and cousins, as well as our friends and all the customers of the Burton Arms. They had all missed our little tribe and after hearing all the tales of lacking luxuries and misadventures could not understand how we managed to survive under such 'spartan hostile conditions'.

But despite the lack of modern amenities and all its quirky dangers, I believe Vicki spoke for us all when she asked, as they all skipped along beside me after Brad's final check-up, "Does that mean we can go home to Africa now Mummy?"

If you enjoyed 'Into Africa', please consider leaving a review.
Thank you!

Preview of 'Still in Africa'

"Mummy, I'm going to be sick."

Here we go again, I thought.

"Brad, is this the 'I'm going to be sick' like when we were on the airplane flying into Africa? But then you weren't sick," I asked. "Or is it like the 'I'm going to be sick' when you actually *were* sick, all down the back of the taxi driver's seat four weeks ago?"

"I don't know, Mummy."

To be on the safe side I reached for the paper bag from the pouch in the aircraft seat in front of me, and handed it to my eldest son.

"Be a good boy and if you think you're going to be sick, be sick in this," I said to him. "Then take it to the nice lady wearing the hat."

I hoped he realised I meant the air stewardess, not the passenger three seats down wearing the colourful turban which matched her African sarong.

I must sound like a dreadful mother, instructing my not yet five-year-old son to dispose of his own sick bag, but one of the things about motherhood I just could not come to grips with, was child vomit. Otherwise my motherly skills weren't so bad, considering I gave birth to twins when Brad was only 17 months old. Three children within eighteen months was quite a challenge.

Taking those children and all your possessions as you accompany your husband to work and live in Africa, is another.

In 1980 my husband Ziggy accepted a two year contract to work in Zambia. When we left England behind we had no idea what to expect, and if we had, I doubt we would have gone. But once we acknowledged and accepted the vagaries of this strange, hot country, and slowed down our inner tempo to fit the dawdling African pace, we found we thoroughly enjoyed it.

During our first year in Kitwe Brad had developed ear problems. Luckily we managed to get Rhinestone, Ziggy's employers, to pay for a midterm return trip to the UK for surgery which was unavailable in Zambia. A lot of things were unavailable in Zambia, but I won't go into that now.

Our sudden, unannounced-appearance at my parents' pub on the 1st August had caused great excitement, though our three and a bit weeks stay seemed very short. It was even shorter for Ziggy, who had to return a week earlier due to pressures of work. No big deal, you'd think. But not so enthralling for me when I had to make the long, three-legged flight back to Zambia on my own with our three small kids.

On the main Heathrow to Lusaka twelve-hour flight we had been allocated seats near the front of economy section. Brad soon discarded his unused sick bag and settled down to fight nicely with his brother and sister. The long, narrow, stainless steel trolley, attended by two Zambian hostesses (as they were called then), had begun its front to back service down the single central aisle, dispensing the customary chicken and beef. I had just returned to my seat after cutting up the kids' food, when Brad hit me with his next blow.

"Mummy, I need a wee."

"Well, it can wait until you've eaten your dinner," I told him.

"It can't, Mummy."

"Yes, it can. Get on with your dinner."

I think he managed two spoonfuls of rice before, "Mummy, I really, REALLY need a wee."

I asked the man next to me if he would be so kind as to hold my tray while I extricated myself from my seat, then held it under his nose so he had no choice. Once out, I repositioned the little fold-down table for my food, onto which he placed my tray, none too gently, before returning his attention to his own dinner.

Putting Brad's meal on my seat, I got him out of his and walked to the nearest hostess, who was serving food to people three rows back.

"I'm terribly sorry," I said, "but my little boy urgently needs to go to the toilet. Would you mind bringing your trolley up this way, just for a moment, so that we can get past?"

"No. He will have to wait," she replied.

"But it really IS urgent."

"Try First Class," she said, then turned away. "Chicken or beef?"

"Bloody charming," I muttered, and turned back to Brad. Time for plan B.

"OK, Sunshine, let's try up here," I said to my son.

Taking him by the hand, I approached the beige curtain which separated us from First Class and peeked through.

I could see the toilet just on the other side of the aircraft's First Class galley, and crept towards it, ushering Brad in front of me. I'd got him inside and was just about to close the door when a harsh voice called out.

"What do you think you are doing here?"

The hostess ran up and pushed me away from the door, when she noticed Brad. She grabbed his hand and pulled him out of the cubicle.

"You cannot use this toilet. You are not First Class passengers!" she hissed, as she shoved us back to the curtain.

"You cannot come through this curtain. It is private to First Class passengers only, and you are not first class!"

I tried to explain to her that he was just a little boy who urgently needed the toilet, and that we couldn't reach the toilets in Economy for ages due to the trolley service.

"That is not my problem."

And with a swish and flurry of cloth, the curtain closed. We were dismissed.

Now I was getting cross.

"Mummeeeeee," wailed Brad "I have to GO."

Time for Plan C.

I returned to the trolley dollies who were now five rows further down the aircraft, but still nowhere near half way along.

"Excuse me, we weren't allowed to use the First Class toilets. Could you please just pass my son over to your colleague and he will take himself to the toilet at the back?" I picked Brad up to pass him to her.

"I am busy," she said. Then, "Chicken or beef?"

So I held Brad up to shoulder level and called out, "Could any passenger back there please take this child off me so that he can go to the toilet?"

After a short delay, which seemed to go on forever holding a 4-year-old child in the air, a man stood up to take him.

I stretched as far as I could, somewhat hindered by the hostess and loaded trolley. Just at the moment of handover, the trolley dolly on the bloke's side turned from her chicken & beefing to find a child in her face, and in the moment of surprise, knocked Brad with her shoulder. All efforts by myself and the knight in shining armour to hold Brad aloft were in vain, and Brad tumbled from our grip.

But he didn't fall far, just right onto the head of a lady in a seat between us, who had just removed the lid from her chicken curry. Brad squeaked and the woman screamed as she stared down at the chicken curry spread all over the front of her dress.

"I'm terribly sorry," I said to the poor woman, "but blame the cabin crew for this. They refused to help in any way. I'm really sorry this happened to you."

She glared at the mess and then at me.

"You should have made the child wait!" she shouted.

I went back to my seat, not feeling in the least bit guilty now about her discomfort. With an attitude like that, I figured she must have had it coming.

It was about 15 minutes before Brad returned from the toilet, having been made to wait until all the meals had been served to the rest of the passengers. He then rushed back to me.

"Everybody was really nice back there, Mummy. People kept asking me if I was all right, and wanted to know what happened, so I told 'em. They thought it was ever so funny!"

The remainder of the flight was uneventful, but strangely lacking in cabin service. So when I wanted a drink I simply walked down to the rear galley, opened the cupboards till I found what I wanted, and took it back to my seat. None of the crew said a word.

To be informed about Ann Patras's new releases, please email
Annpatras.author@gmail.com
Contact welcome!

About the author

Ann Patras was born and raised in Burton upon Trent in the English Midlands. Her life was always crammed with people, originally through her family's busy corner shop, then at her parents' pub and through her own varied careers.

After raising three kids, countless dogs and living in Africa for over thirty years, Ann and Ziggy, almost 40 years married, now live in Andalucia, Spain and have absolutely no intention of moving again.

Contacts and Links

Email
Annpatras.author@gmail.com

Blog - The Crazy World of Ann Patras
http://annpatrasauthor.com

Ann Patras on Facebook
https://www.facebook.com/ann.patrasauthor?ref=ts&fref=ts

The 'Africa' Series on Facebook
https://www.facebook.com/AnnPatrasAfricaSeries?fref=ts

Acknowledgements

Initial thanks must go to my cousin Tony Johnson, who helped me set up my first PC for the sole purpose of writing this book back in 1987. (Unfortunately, many more computers were harmed in the process of producing this book.)

Sadly my family has dwindled away over the years, but I would like to thank the remaining stalwarts for their support: Bernard and Rita Johnson, Paul & Paula Johnson, Jean Hackett (Elson), and Jady Glauds. Also my assorted cousins, etc. too numerous to mention.

Thanks must go to the multitudes of friends who continually asked, "Ann, when are you going to finish writing that book?"

- Originating in Burton upon Trent – Cathy Disney, Bill & Pat Sales, Aileen O'Shea, Pat Dennis (Elliott), and Di Dicks (Hobson) now in Canada.

- My supporters from Africa – ranging from a few still living in Zambia, some in Zimbabwe and lots down in South Africa. Unfortunately too many to name for fear of missing any.

- I need to thank my special friend and fellow author, Irene Hamilton, in Grand Prairie, Canada who has been a huge supporter, yet whom I haven't even met!

- And of course I cannot miss out my new (and some very old) supporters now living in Spain – several being ex-Af-exPats. A special thanks must go to John Holland for helping me conquer the basic mysteries of Photoshop editing and to Colin Leek for his innovative formatting suggestion and general help.

There must be to be a special thank you to James Clark, columnist and author of plenty in Johannesburg, for his encouragement to 'keep at it'.

And another very special thank you must be given to my spectacularly wonderful, beautiful, talented, she-told-me-to-say-all-this, absolutely awesome publisher

Victoria Twead for her hard work and dedication to my cause. She is a slave-driver of note.

The biggest THANK YOU simply has go to my three perfect, incredibly awesome (and now quite old) 'kids', Brad Anthony, Victoria and Leon James, who have encouraged me every single step of the way. They even consented to my using their given names, as the *S*T*A*R*S* of Into Africa, (without realizing what I am going to be disclosing in 'Staying in Africa', and subsequent books. Idiots!)

Last, but not least, I cannot leave out the one responsible for all this malarkey in the first place – the long standing love of my life and husband of 40 years, Ziggy. Thanks pal, this is all down to YOU!

Ann Patras

2014

CPSIA information can be obtained at www.ICGtesting.com
Printed in the USA
LVOW11s1613300714

396752LV00004B/739/P